GUITAR CLUES
operation pentatonic

by greg koch

ISBN-13: 978-0-634-07414-1
ISBN-10: 1-634-07414-8

HAL•LEONARD®
CORPORATION

7777 W. BLUEMOUND RD. P.O. BOX 13819 MILWAUKEE, WI 53213

In Australia Contact:
Hal Leonard Australia Pty. Ltd.
4 Lentara Court
Cheltenham, Victoria, 3192 Australia
Email: ausadmin@halleonard.com

Visit Hal Leonard Online at
www.halleonard.com

CONTENTS

INTRODUCTION

What clues?" you may ask. Well, my friends, instead of just bombarding you with a deluge of theory and a myriad of scales, both of which usually numb the average soul into a state of self-deprecating perplexity (often exemplified by a vacuous expression and a dab of drool around the corners of the mouth), I will "clue" you in to a bevy of tasty morsels which you can immediately apply to lead and/or rhythm playing, which will inspire you to play better guitar. What a concept!

By taking one of the most basic improvisatory tools, the pentatonic scale, and employing all the powers of minutia, you shall accumulate a host of ideas and nuances that, demonstrated in sample improvisations over guitar rhythm tracks which are also transcribed, will have you playing more inspired lead and rhythm guitar from the first few pages. Whether you are somewhat new to improvising or have been doing it for a while, you will harvest golden info-nuggets that you can put to use right away, from volume swells to chicken-pickin' to intervallic and chordal ideas. All of these things are shown in a universally-applicable bluesy environment that gradually adds cool skills to basic concepts, which not only makes it easy to use effectively right away but also makes it easy to explain to others, if you are so inclined. A host of other facts and tidbits are thrown in to clue you in on everything from keeping your guitar in tune to jam etiquette inspired by the onslaught of questions received by the author at clinics, at gigs, and on the internet. This is not a beginner's book, nor is it a grand thesis on improvisatory complexity, but folks on both ends of the spectrum can learn something from it!

Enough of this slathering of propaganda, let's get involved!

The Minor Pentatonic Scale

The majority of our learning will be in the key of A, which is centrally located on the neck at the fifth fret, and once the skills in question are understood they can be deployed in any key of your choosing by simply moving your hand to the appropriate fret. The A minor pentatonic scale is a classic example of a visual "box" pattern that the novice can quickly reference as a safe zone for improvisatory activity, and is also a great tool for those who are looking to simplify their lead guitar approach. We'll get it on by playing **only** the notes in the scale for the duration of a solo in a tune or a vamp centered around A7 or A minor, particularly a twelve-bar blues in either A major or minor.

The minor pentatonic scale consists of five notes which, of course, puts the "pent" in pentatonic. These five notes in A minor are A–C–D–E–G. After you play those five notes in the lower octave, ya keep on going in that position until you run out of notes!

Here is the scale in the 5th-fret position.

TRACK 2

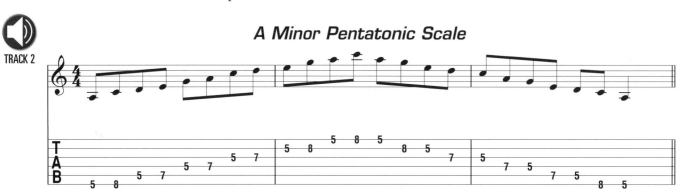

A Minor Pentatonic Scale

You can see by this diagram how this box scale shape corresponds to an A barre chord at the 5th fret, thereby providing a handy-dandy safe zone for soloing.

A Minor Pentatonic Diagram

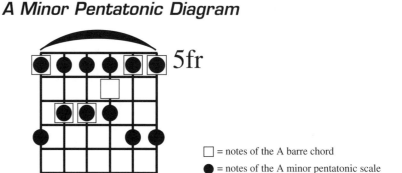

☐ = notes of the A barre chord
● = notes of the A minor pentatonic scale

Some frown on this visual approach, and certainly as you progress you'll want your hands to do your ears' bidding, but you have to stumble before you can run, and your eyes can do for you now what your ears will do for you later!

Slides

Let's add a little seasoning to this scale before I give you a sample improvisation, with a quick slide from a half step (one fret) above or a half step below your target note. Jazz players employ slides more often than bends, as they are more stylistically correct in mainstream jazz, probably because sets of flatwound strings with a wound G string make bending a little dicey. Rest assured, jazz pioneers like Lonnie Johnson, Eddie Lang, Django Reinhardt, and Charlie Christian bent strings with great aplomb, but somewhere along the line the jazz police passed laws against the string benders and they were forbidden to shake them strings (probably because the horn players knew that the guitar would soon rule the world if allowed the opportunity!). Be that as it may, sliding is a very effective little nuance, so try these two exercises.

In the first exercise you start by fingering a note a half step **below** the target note in the scale. After playing this first note you immediately slide **up** (to the higher pitch) by dragging your finger up the neck, keeping pressure on the string as your finger glides over the fret.

A Minor Pentatonic Scale with Ascending Slides

In the second exercise you start by fingering a note a half step **above** the desired note, and drag your finger **down** the neck, maintaining pressure as your finger glides over the fret.

A Minor Pentatonic Scale with Descending Slides

I have chosen blues progressions for the majority of the sample improvisations because I feel the basis for any good improviser in pret' near any idiom is a strong foundation in the blues. The ability to emote over a simple set of chords while being conversational with a concept of dynamics separates the musically articulate from the noodlers!

Slidin' and Shufflin'

 **Lead**

This example is a juicy little shuffle groove, which I'll get into in more detail when we talk about the rhythm track. The sample improvisation employs slides which I intentionally overused for demonstration purposes. I do some quick slides up and down to get a bluesy slurred effect, and the use of triplets, hammer-ons, and pull-offs really help create a *vibe* (if I can digress into some hip jargon—for the kids).

I was going for a Kenny Burrell-type thing on this tune (if you don't own any Kenny Burrell, shame on you, but you can redeem yourself by getting his release *Midnight Blue* on the Bluenote label). Although Kenny played a big archtop guitar, I was just using the neck pickup on my Fender Custom Shop Strat that I've had forever, which is basically a hot-rodded '56 with Fender Custom Shop Fat '50s pickups in the neck and middle positions, and a Seymour Duncan JB Junior in the bridge. I was plugged into the Cyber Twin SE with my "Spank That Thang" setting that is hard-wired on the amp, but I modified the sound by turning the volume up to 7 and the gain down to 4½. I turned off the delay and rolled back the volume a hair on the guitar. It is basically a Fender '59 Bassman setting with a little Black Face-era reverb. I use this setting for the lion's share of the CD.

Listen through the example first and then play along with it when you are comfortable. If you want to learn it note for note, cool and the gang. If you just want to pilfer the licks you think are cool, let the good times roll. Throughout this book, use these sample improvisations in any way you see fit. The chord symbols shown here are just basic seventh chords outlining the 12-bar form. See the rhythm part which follows for more detailed chord voicings.

When playing this, however, be aware of the dynamics (the change in volume created by picking softer or harder). The art of saying the most with the least amount of notes—or note choices, in this instance—can depend greatly on the attack from one note to the next. This is where the ears have to hear nuances that are deceptive because of the relative simplicity of the note choices. Digging in with the pick some places while being more sensitive in others will certainly assist you in your quest.

TRACK 5

Moderate Shuffle ♩ = 120

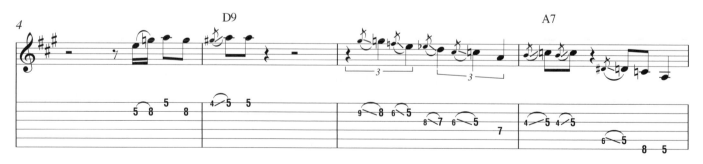

Rhythm

Now, let's suss the rhythm pattern of this piece before messing around with some improvisation over the jam track. It is always good to know what is going on underneath you while soloing, so let's get 'er done before the jamming can commence!

Playing rhythm, or *comping* (accompanying) as the jazz cats like to call it, is something that a lot of folks who simply want to exercise fretboard conflagration overlook, much to their undoing in the real world of professional musicianship. A guitarist who can lend sinewy rhythmic accompaniment to any musical environment is worth his/her weight in gold. (A certain Keith Richards comes to mind.) This is why I thought it was important to transcribe the rhythm parts throughout the book as well as the leads, so that you are able to add to your rhythm chops in addition to adding to your ability to noodle like a bold warrior in the lead department.

This rhythm part exemplifies a shuffle pattern that fuses a raunchy blues-guitar approach with a jazzy organ player's mindset not unlike Hendrix's strummery on "Rainy Day, Dream Away" off his *Electric Ladyland* release. As witnesses have reported, Hendrix was going for a Kenny Burrell feel on that track and that, fused with his more hardcore blues savvy, created something from which the world has yet to fully recover!

The shuffle rhythm on this bad boy is achieved by an up-and-down strumming pattern that is made more percussive by a combination of picking-hand, palm-, and fretting-hand muting achieved by lessening pressure on the strings so that the axe is little more than a very expensive, percussive washboard of a sort, as in the second half of beat 1 of measure 1.

There is a triple-stop (a three-note chord) with vibrato that certainly conveys a sense of girth to this little piece as in the fourth beat of measure 1. This is best achieved by using the third finger of your fretting hand and giving the strings a little shake, by applying pressure and bringing all three strings down toward the floor first, then back to their original position, doing all in rapid succession.

I have transcribed the main rhythm pattern, or what I feel is the most important part of it. Had I transcribed every one of the rhythm patterns on the accompanying CD from start to finish, this book would closely resemble *War and Peace* in thickness, and the time it would have taken would have caused my wife to declare war, and I would never again know peace. Fear not, the main gist is here!

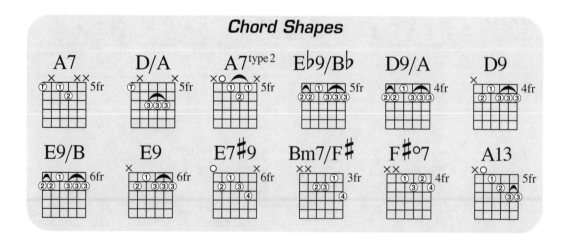

Moderate Shuffle ♩ = 120

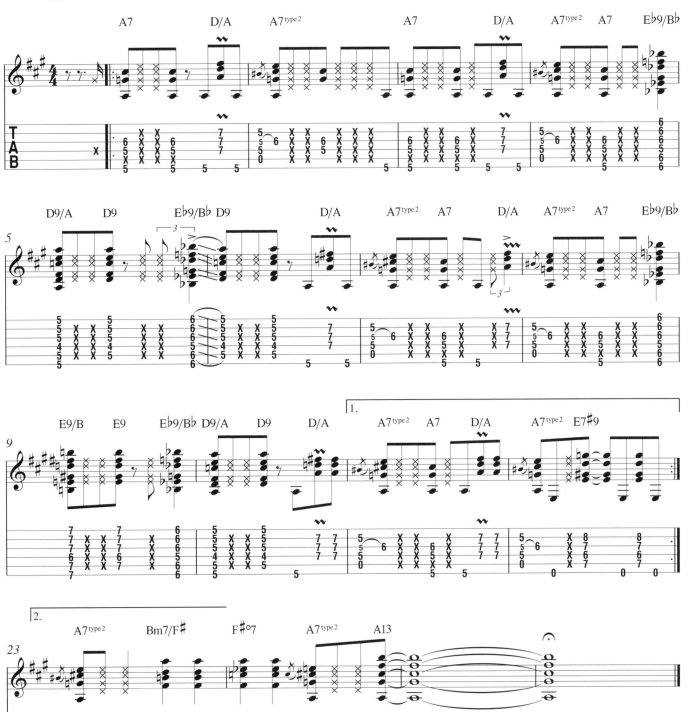

 Once you can comfortably play the rhythm pattern, take a stab at improvising a solo over Track 6. Try to exhaustively explore the sliding skills discussed so far, saving your bends for the next lesson.

BENDING

Although I think it's safe to say that the half-step bend is much easier to tackle right out of the gate, I have chosen to skip ahead to an exercise that has you bending each note of our A minor pentatonic scale up a whole step and then back down again. Before we just trudge ahead with this exercise, here are a few pointers for those of you who experience both psychological and physical pain when trying to bend strings.

Everyone always asks me about string gauges when the subject of string-bending comes up, and the bottom line is: whatever works for you. I personally use a .010-.046 set of Stainless Steel Fender Bullet strings on the ol' Strat. I used to use a .009-.046 set but I personally feel that a bigger string sounds a little better, is less likely to break, and stays in tune a little better. Having said that, there are a lot of folks out there who feel compelled to use heavy strings (like a set starting with .012 or .013 on the high E string) because they have read that Stevie Ray Vaughan and others use these gauges to achieve their monstrous tones. To many, it's a badge of machismo to use heavy strings. I have two responses to that notion. One, a guitar tuned downed to E♭ with heavy-gauged strings, with big ol' frets on it, feels just like a guitar with medium-jumbo frets tuned to standard pitch with a set of .010's. Two, if your bending sounds like a waterfowl about to be sacrificed to the gods of mediocrity, or you are contemplating the use of steroids to build up strength in your fretting hand so that you can shake them strings with a little more facility, you need to step away from the edge and put on lighter strings.

The first picture below is a traditional fretting-hand grip, where the fingers look more vertical on the fretboard like pistons ready to pounce, with the thumb located on the back of the neck. In the second picture, the thumb is draped over the top of the neck, giving you a little more strength to bend, assisted by the fingers assuming more of a horizontal slant.

Traditional Fretting-Hand Position

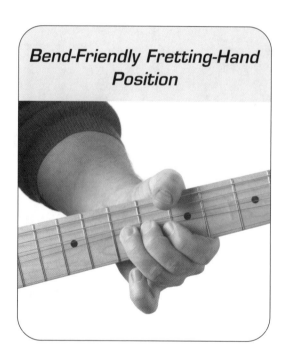

Bend-Friendly Fretting-Hand Position

As a general rule, I bend the E, A, and D strings down (towards the ground) and the G, B, and high E strings up, toward the sky. There are the occasions where this rule is subject to change in regard to the D and G strings, but for now, adhere to the rule for ease in bending.

With these things in mind, give Track 7 a try.

A Minor Pentatonic Scale with String Bending

VIBRATO

Here we go, to the meat of the matter: vibrato. Vibrato is the mirror to the soul. Well, maybe that's a little extreme, but suffice it to say, vibrato, as done with the fretting hand, is what gives a guitarist his/her identity. Ok, maybe that's a little much as well, so let's just say vibrato is flippin' sweet. Now that we have that out of the way, let's look into how to do it.

The search for good vibrato can take some to the mountains of Tibet to find the Dalai Lama for spiritual enlightenment while others come to it easily by settling for a vibrato that sounds like a well-caffeinated chipmunk. I use a variety of different vibratos depending on the feeling I'm trying to evince, so the one demonstrated here is not VIBRATO, period, but rather an example of a believable vibrato. The quest to refine and expand one's catalog of vibratos is never-ending. You will constantly hear other players whose vibratos knock you out, or you may hear yourself on a recording and be repulsed to the point of wanting to redefine your playing, vibrato and all. That is why it is good to record yourself a lot: so that you can scrutinize your vibrato and playing in general to correct and refine as you go. Something I suggest to people who are just trying vibrato for the first time is if you are using a guitar with a whammy bar, use the bar to emulate different types of vibrato first and then immediately try to replicate it with your fingers.

The mechanics of actually achieving vibrato with the fingers of your fretting hand varies depending on the vibrato that you are trying to achieve. Classical and jazz players achieve a traditional guitar vibrato by shaking the finger back and forth horizontally on the fretboard (parallel to the line of the string) while maintaining pressure with the tip of the finger. The finger is more piston-like due to the traditional grip I alluded to earlier.

The blues/rock vibrato is a much more vertical maneuver in terms of actually moving the string up and down (perpendicular to the string), raising the pitch slightly and then bringing it back. Since the blues/rock grip on the neck (with the thumb draped over the top, etc.) has the fingers slanted in a slightly horizontal approach to the fretboard, you don't typically use the very tip of your finger to get this vibrato but off-center of your fingertip pad, if you will. This area will be a little sensitive as you will be bending the string with this part of your finger to get the vibrato. Try not to squeeze the neck harder than usual when applying vibrato. Most of the added energy should go into the up and down movement of the string rather than straight into the fretboard. This will reduce the wear on your fingers and the frets. With practice your hand will learn what to do and less effort will be required.

I find that it is much easier to get consistent vibrato on all strings (except the high E) by bending the string downward first to bring the pitch up slightly, then releasing it back down to its original pitch, and repeating (obviously). With the high E string you have to push the string up first to alter the pitch, then bring it down to its original pitch. For either the high or low E string, you have to be careful so as not to drag the string off the fretboard. Vibrato is always a challenge in the beginning but, again, with perseverance, you will get 'er.

Eric Clapton's vibrato has been sublime throughout his career but watching him achieve it is mind-numbing. He pushes up first regardless of string, making his vibrato a little more difficult to control. I went through a phase where I had to get the Clapton thang happening, and I still alternate between pushing up first and pulling down to achieve vibrato, but I think that in the beginning it is probably easier to try going down first on all strings but the high E.

Your approach to vibrato can vary depending on which finger you are using. B.B. King has an example of vibrato that is particularly effective when using the first finger. It's called the "butterfly" vibrato because your hand looks like a butterfly fluttering to and fro. Applying pressure with your first finger on the string, shake your hand back and forth at the wrist while extending your thumb and pinky out like the wings of a butterfly. Your hand should look like you're shaking a top hat as you sing, "Hello my baby, hello my honey, hello my ragtime gal..." That's a little obscure but I think you know what I mean. The butterfly vibrato won't work on the high E string, as you will drag the string right off the fretboard.

Mind you, all these are merely suggestions. Remember my rule: that there are no rules other than "whatever it takes"—when it comes to guitar playing, anyway.

Now, take a stab at this example, applying vibrato to the notes of the minor pentatonic scale.

A Minor Pentatonic Scale with Vibrato

TRACK 8

BENDS WITH VIBRATO

Combining bends with vibrato is, again, a skill that you are never done refining. You need to apply all of the previous discussions in your quest for musicality in this regard. The only other suggestion I have for the next exercise is that you bend the string up to the desired pitch *before* adding vibrato.

Notice in this example that bending each note of A minor pentatonic up a whole step gives us the same notes as the **B** minor pentatonic scale. In other words, we need to remember that bending a note changes its musical pitch. In the soloing examples, you'll find I don't bend the root of the scale up very often (from A to B). Instead I'd usually bend *up to the root* from a whole step below (G to A).

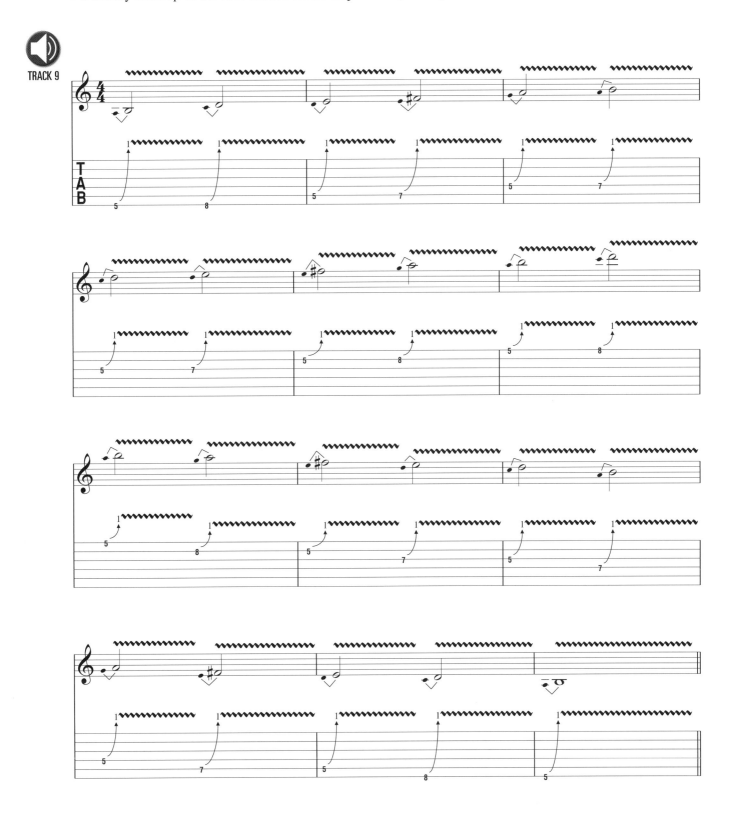

Bend 'em and Shake 'em

 **Lead**

This piece combines bending and vibrato over a minor blues in the key of A. I keep it pretty simple so as to not drive you cuckoo. I incorporate the vibratos of some of my favorites, particularly Albert King, Otis Rush, and there's always a dash of Jimi in there for good measure. If you don't have any Albert King, any of his Stax-era recordings will get you in the ballpark. My favorite Otis Rush selections are from a compilation record called *Chicago: The Blues Today!* If you can find a live version of Hendrix doing "Red House" from the Albert Hall show in 1969, originally released on the record *Hendrix in the West* and subsequently included on various CD compilations, you will hear one of the greatest blues guitar performances of all time.

The sounds on this piece were created with the same gear and settings as the previous one. All right, now give this beast a try and then we will look at the rhythm track.

TRACK 10

Medium Funk ♩ = 93

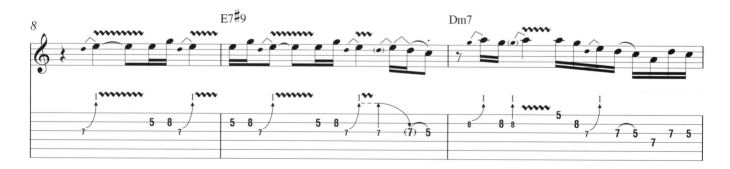

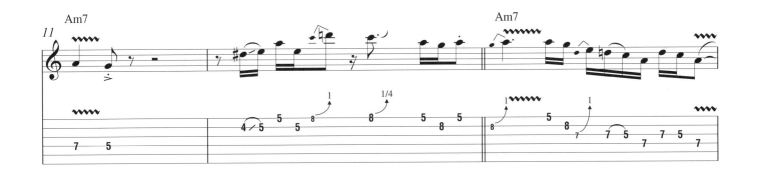

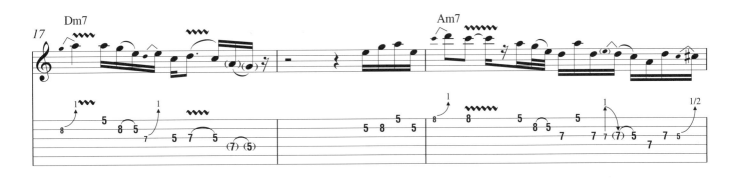

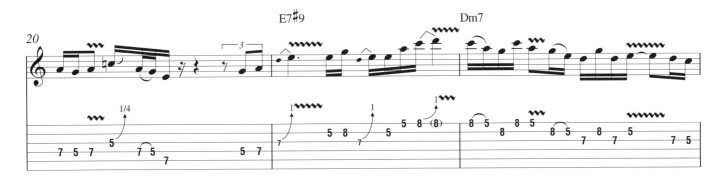

Bend 'em and Shake 'em - Lead

 **Rhythm**

The main rhythm part here is a combination of Hendrix nuggets and other little chordal riffs I have lifted from anyone from Steve Cropper to Prince. This is a typical minor blues progression, probably made most famous by B.B. King's "The Thrill Is Gone." As in the "Slidin' and Shufflin' " piece earlier, there are a lot of muted percussive accents in this piece. Bring these out by using a combination of palm muting with your picking hand and loosening the grip with your fretting hand here and there to mute as you strum. All the other nuances should be self-explanatory with the transcription and the track, with the exception of the conga effect, which I'll explain after you get the main rhythm part.

Chord Shapes

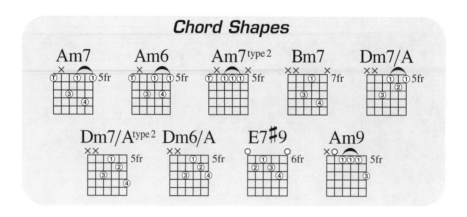

TRACK 11

Medium Funk ♩ = 93

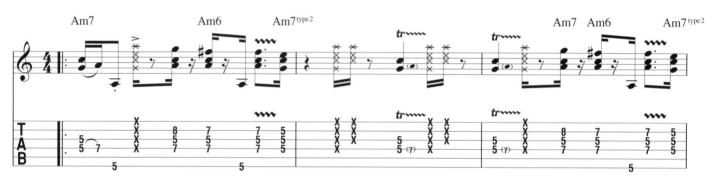

*Play this rhythm on beat 2 of repeat.

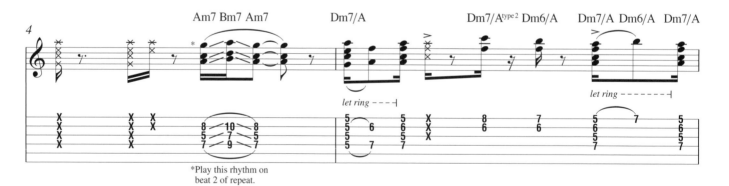

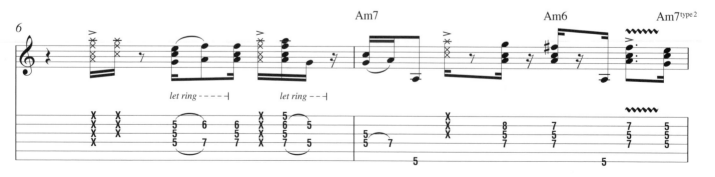

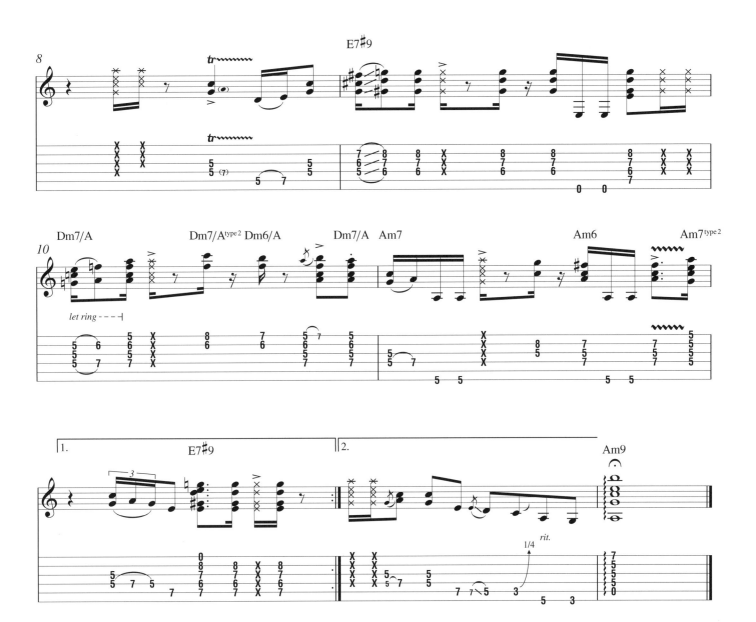

CONGA EFFECT

This is just a fun little thing to throw in when you want to add a little extra percussive activity. All I did here was mute the strings entirely with my fretting hand somewhere about halfway up the neck, and use my picking-hand thumb to tap the low E string at the 12th fret for the low conga and, again with the thumb, tap the D and G strings at the 15th fret to get the high conga sound. Give it a try!

TRACK 12

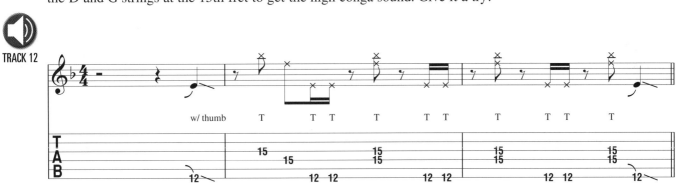

PINCH HARMONICS

Probably the most famous example of pinch harmonics is Billy Gibbons's outro solo on the ZZ Top tune "La Grange," but I think the first one to really make his mark with the pinch harmonic as a stylistic tool was the late Telecaster master, Roy Buchanan. If you haven't heard any Roy you will want to pick up his first record, just entitled *Roy Buchanan* (Polydor), or get his release called *Livestock*. That should bring you up to speed. As a side note, when listening to these older recordings, one should always consider the era and what was being done for the first time that we may take for granted now.

Making a pinch harmonic sound right can be a little tricky. It can be easier to achieve if you are playing with a lot of distortion, with the bridge pickup of your guitar. Telecasters set to the bridge pickup don't even need distortion to really be effective with pinch harmonics as ol' Roy Buchanan would attest to. Basically, you want to choke way up on your pick so that barely any of the pick is visible, and as you pick a note with a downstroke, the string, after being struck with your pick, is immediately hit with the side of the thumb on your picking hand. This will cause the pinch harmonic to sound (an overtone, usually an octave and a 5th above the actual pitch). It's like you are pinching the sound out between the pick and your thumb—hence the name (though you do not literally grab the string as if you were pinching somebody).

The following example is a pinch harmonic bend with vibrato. For some reason, I find it a little easier to show people pinch harmonics in conjunction with a bend. I switched to the bridge pickup (Seymour Duncan JB Junior) on my Strat with the volume full up for this, but the amp setting was the same as before. Try it. If no overtone comes out, try attacking the string in a slightly different place, a little closer to or farther from the bridge. It takes practice and a bit of experimentation.

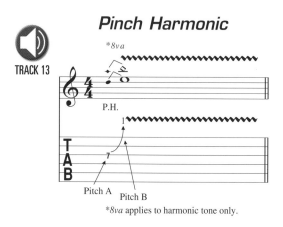

Pinch Harmonic

TRACK 13

*8va applies to harmonic tone only.

Also try raking the pick down through the low strings (muted with your picking hand palm) until you strike the intended string with the pick held in the way described above to achieve the pinch harmonic.

The amp setting for the following example was changed to a variation of the Blues Combo setting on the Cyber Twin SE. This is a cyber recreation of the old Marshall JTM 45 combo amp that Eric Clapton used on the John Mayall's *Blues Breakers* record that everyone crows about (for good reason). Whatever you use to get the distortion, the example should sound something like this.

Pinch Harmonic with Distorted Tone

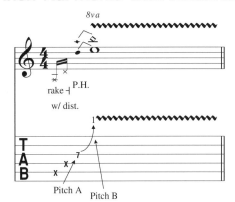

The next exercise has you playing all the notes of the A minor pentatonic scale position we have learned thus far in pinch harmonics. Having a little distortion on your amp and using the bridge pickup on your guitar will get you in the zone. Play along with the example until you can replicate it. The harmonic pitches shown here are not exact, but represent common overtone pitches produced by pinch harmonics. This, like anything, is not impossible, but takes time!

Pinch Harmonics in Eighth Notes

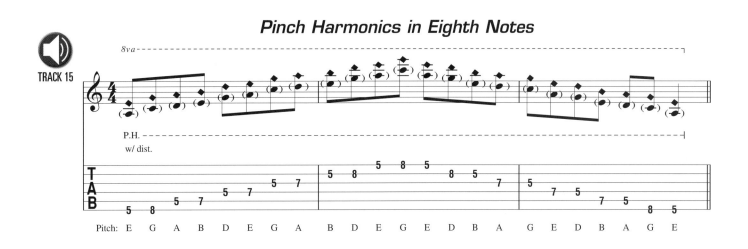

Pinch It

This next piece is very ZZ Top-ish, which is never a bad thing, as they are bona fide blues demons who turn it up to 11. The lead part uses all the skills we have learned thus far, with only the notes of the A minor pentatonic scale. The gear and settings are the same as on the previous pinch-harmonic examples.

There is lots of slovenly, muted string-raking for effect in this tune which gives the lead a greasy percussive attack. This is offset by the squeals of the pinch harmonics. Feel free to curl your upper lip in a rock-pig grimace when playing this selection. Turn it up!

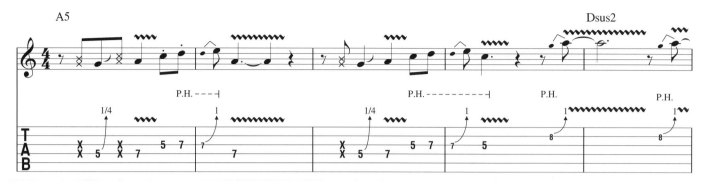

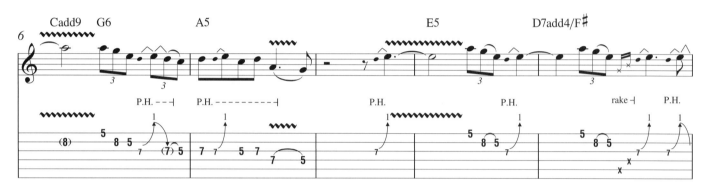

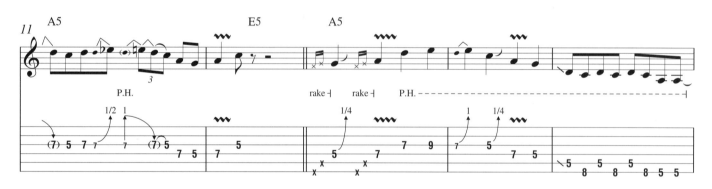

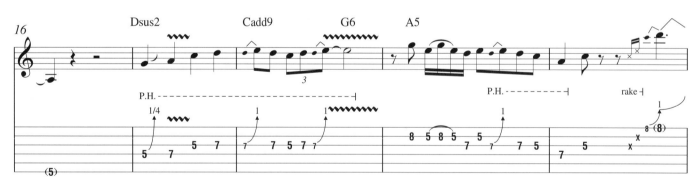

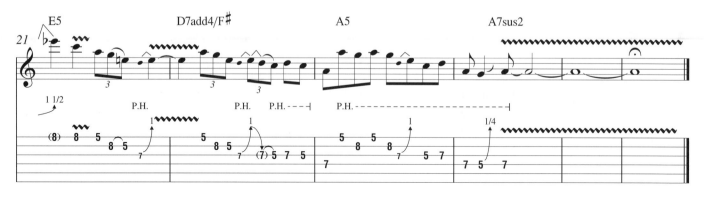

Rhythm

This rhythm part uses chords with open strings, all done in the first position area of the neck of the git-fiddle. Some distortion is needed to get the grit necessary to make this riff come alive. A little vibrato on the G string on the "A" riff will rock your world, and when playing that D chord with the descending bass notes, let them strings ring, loud and proud.

Chord Shapes

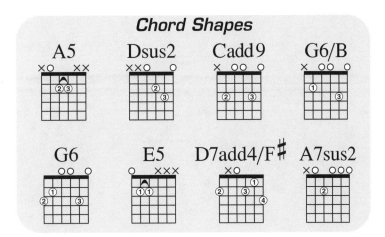

TRACK 17

Moderate Shuffle ♩ = 121

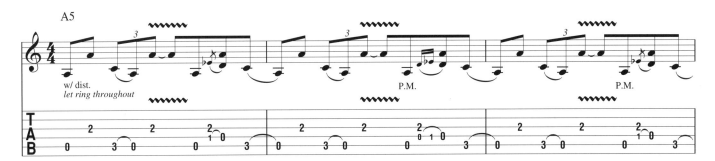

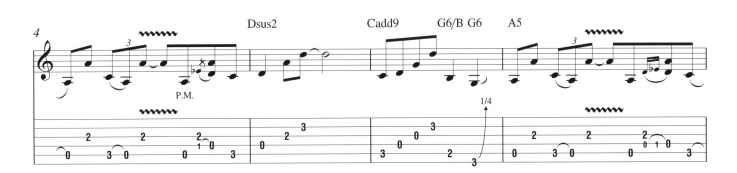

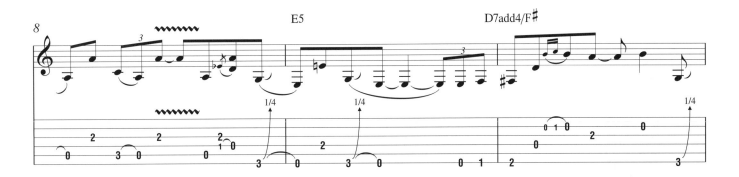

 Now, use the tools you have picked up so far and jam over the rhythm track to "Pinch It" (Track 17). Don't be afraid to pinch-harmonic yourself into oblivion—it's good clean fun. It may be necessary to maintain the aforementioned curled lip to pull this off.

Scale Manipulation

"Manipulation" sounds kind of unsavory, but I'm referring to taking the notes of our A minor pentatonic scale and using them in different ways to give you a variety of melodic ideas for soloing. We will pick apart the scale, breaking it up by intervals, and as in the following exercise, by a repeating note sequence. It is important to get these exercises off the paper and under your fingers—memorized—as quickly as possible so that you can practice them at will. When the sounds get ingrained in your brain they will eventually make the transition from exercises into real improvisatory material for you on down the line. Playing the exercises in time to a metronome, with your foot tapping **steadily** (the opposite of willy-nilly), is essential to this incorporation process.

Check out the first exercise. It takes the scale in six-note bursts, ascending and then descending. The ascending groups start with the index finger on your fretting hand. When descending, start with the pinky on the first two six-note groups, and start with the ring finger for the second two. All notes are to be picked using alternate picking—you know, strictly up-and-down—as opposed to down, down, up, down, up, up or any such permutation.

You may want to employ a little palm muting for effect as you speed it up. The track demonstrates the exercise first in eighth-note triplets (three notes per click of the metronome), then in septuplets as written (exactly twice as fast: six notes per click). This is a useful improv tool at either speed.

Pentatonic Scale in Groups of Six

TRACK 18

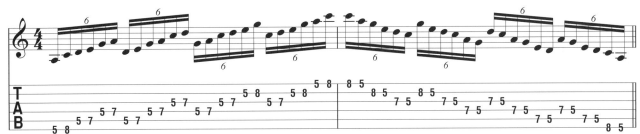

2nds... Kind Of

If we were using the major scale (that "do-re-mi" thing with seven notes in it), this next exercise would consist of only major 2nd (two frets) or minor 2nd (one fret) intervals. That's why I say "kind of." We're applying the exercise to the pentatonic scale, which means that some of the notes are actually a minor 3rd (three frets) apart.

We start on the second note of the scale, then descend to the root. That's it. Those first two notes define the pattern. To continue it, we start on the third note of the scale and descend to the second. Repeat until you run out of notes in the position. Then do it backwards (ascending groups of two notes) as you work your way back down the scale. It may not seem like a big deal, but when you get it going you will be doing something you may not have done much of before, which is playing notes on the same fret but different strings by rolling your fingertips.

The track demonstrates the exercise first in half notes (one note lasts for two clicks), then in quarter notes (one note per click), and finally in eighth notes (two notes per click).

Remember—alternate picking!

Pentatonic Scale in Groups of Two, Stepwise Motion

Pickin' and Pullin'

This funky little ditty incorporates some speedy alternate-picking snippets and some hammer-on-pull-off salvos utilizing our recent acquisitions of the ideas from the last two exercises. In addition, there is plenty of bending, vibrato, and sliding.

I overstate the use of the intervals and scalar ideas for the purpose of example so you'll have to forgive me if this is a little over the top. Amongst the speedy lickery, there are some slower Albert King-ish blues licks in here for ya.

The tone on this tune was achieved with the same settings and rig as "Shufflin and Slidin'." Now, let's pick it and pull it!

TRACK 20

Moderate Funk ♩ = 121

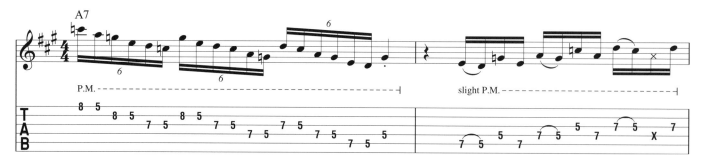

Rhythm

The main rhythm part on this tune is a skanky little seventh-chord groove that is a hybrid of the chord stylings of Leo Nocentelli from the Meters, and Steve Cropper, the legendary axeman from Booker T. & the MG's. Again, if you don't have any of their stuff, I'm gonna give ya what for, but you can redeem yourself by purchasing some of their material with much haste and eagerness.

The funkification is a brought to the fore here by savage strumming with a little bit of picking-hand palm muting on the high-string passages. This really makes the chords percolate. The basic sixteenth strum pattern is shown in the notation, but you'll hear on the recording how I vary the rhythm and the placement of the chord stabs from time to time. The chordal trills (a nice one pops out in measure 3) are a little tricky, but they are worth it. Instead of trying to bring both fingers up and down at the same time, you can try sliding back and forth; it should make it a little easier.

The tone is the same as I used for the lead with the exception of the combination of the neck and middle pickup as opposed to just the neck.

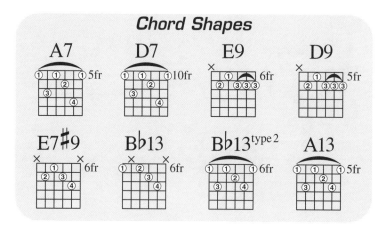

TRACK 21

Moderate Funk ♩ = 121

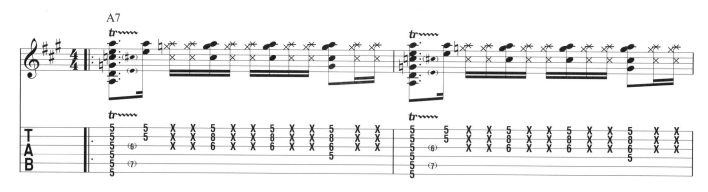

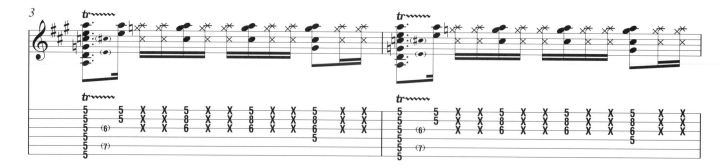

 Now it is time for you to take a stab at soloing on "Pickin' and Pullin'." Try to incorporate the 2nds and the other scalar idea, along with the other skills we have deployed thus far, as you play over Track 21.

4THS... MOSTLY

The minor pentatonic scale can be played in perfect 4th intervals, with the exception of one major 3rd that appears when combining its second scale degree with the fourth scale degree. Other than that, when we play the scale in this manner, up and down, the sound of the fourths is solidly identifiable.

Note that like in the 2nds exercise, when we get to the highest note, we play the two-note pattern backwards, this time switching from higher note first, lower note second, as we descend. As before, the following tracks are played three times through (half notes, quarter notes, and eighth notes).

Alternate pick!

TRACK 22

Pentatonic Scale in 4ths

The following exercise is exactly the same as the previous one, only the second group is backwards, creating a four-note pattern. It goes up two notes and down the next two. It may be confusing to read about but you'll know what I mean when you play it.

TRACK 23

Pentatonic Scale in Alternating Ascending and Descending 4ths

I don't know when I first heard the term *double stops* but I know I was playing them long before I learned to call them by that name. It simply means a lick or riff that involves playing two notes at the same time. It makes lead and melody lines much thicker.

This next exercise applies double stops to the pentatonic-scale-in-4ths concept. Again, there are a couple of thirds that pop up. This is a delightful device for lead guitar activity and has a unique, quasi-oriental sound to it.

You can fingerpick this exercise by using your thumb on one string and first finger on the other to simultaneously pluck the two strings. You can alternate between that and using your second finger on one string and your third finger on another.

Another cool option is to *hybrid*-pick it by using your pick on one string and your middle finger on another to simultaneously pluck the strings. Alternatively, you can take the way of the sloth and just strum them both with the pick. However, you really can achieve two more-distinct tones if you use one of the above methods.

TRACK 24

Pentatonic Scale in Double-Stop 4ths

A 4th to Be Reckoned with Blues

Lead

Long ago, I was bewitched by the power of Jimi Hendrix. I can say with a degree of certainty that he is one of the main reasons I began playing guitar and he remains a constant source of inspiration for me. If you don't own at least his first three releases (*Are You Experienced*, *Axis: Bold as Love*, and *Electric Ladyland*), you are depriving yourself of the work of an unbridled genius. These are strong words but they have been reiterated by giants in every genre of music. Plainly put, he was a freak of nature.

Why am I saying this now? Because this next minor blues is very Jimi-esque. Although the primary purpose of "A 4th to Be Reckoned with Blues" is to supply a sample improvisation using 4ths, since Jimi was no stranger to using 4ths both in his rhythm playing and in his leads, I gave the piece a little "Jim" flavoring. The lead has some "Jim" to it and the rhythm part really does.

This transcription is pretty self-explanatory. One thing I would like to mention is that when playing the double-stop 4ths, if you choke up on the pick and do a pinch harmonic, you get a very Jimi-esque sound that will provide delight to you and yours.

The same clean amp setting was used as in the previous exercise with the neck pickup on the Strat.

TRACK 25

Rhythm

This tune is basically a minor blues. The minor blues differs chordally from our typical twelve bar blues in that a lot of times you'll have a ♭VI chord (an F major or F7 chord of some sort if the song is in A minor) right before the V (an E or E7). "The Thrill Is Gone" is an excellent example. These two chords afford an improviser some options for variety when soloing that require a little more knowledge of harmony but, rest assured, your trusty friend, the minor pentatonic scale, will get ya thru the tough times!

Before we jam over Track 26, let's talk a little bit about the rhythm pattern. It is Jimi-like, to be sure, but I would be remiss if I did not cite the substantial influence of the guitarist for the Impressions, Curtis Mayfield, on Jimi's playing. The quick hammer-on/pull-off embellishments, the clean, pinch-harmonic-ed double stops and sliding triple stops are all right out of the Mayfield grab bag of rhythmic chording excellence! Jimi expounded on these things, to be sure, as do I on this little ditty.

I want to take a moment to say again that you can use this book any way that you want. You may want to explore every little nook and cranny, or you may just decide you like a little chord lick from this tune and a lead lick from another. It's all good. Don't be put off by a selection that, in its entirety, may seem too hard but may have a little sump'n-sump'n that you can apply immediately.

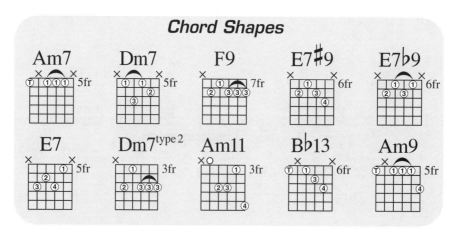

 Now give Track 26 a listen and pilfer what you will!

TRACK 26

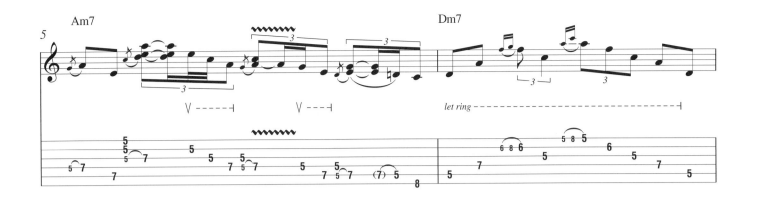

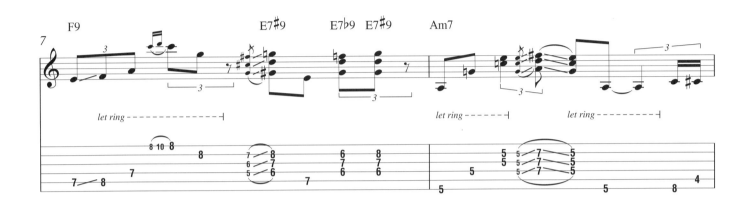

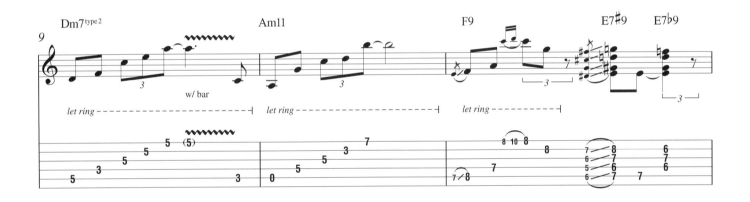

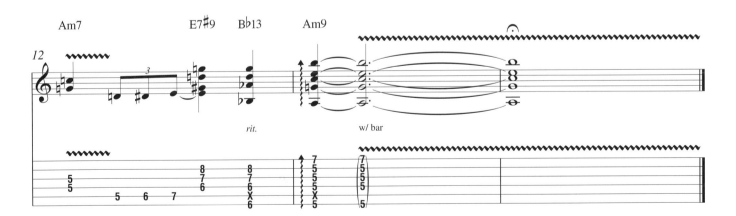

 You know what time it is. Using all the tricks learned so far, throw down over "A 4th to Be Reckoned with Blues," Track 26.

5THS... YES, 5THS

OK. Our minor pentatonic scale can be broken up into perfect 5th intervals (with one minor 6th from E to C), which serve as another delightful option for improvising. The next two exercises take 5ths and approach them in the same way that we did the 4ths. You can alternate-pick these exercises, or, as the gaps between intervals widen, you may think about hybrid picking them, using your pick for one of the notes and your middle finger for the other. This will lead to speed later on.

As with the other interval studies, try to commit these to memory as quickly as possible. Avoid looking repeatedly at the page. Again, the examples are played first in half notes, followed by quarter notes, and finally in eighths as written.

Pentatonic Scale in 5ths

TRACK 27

Pentatonic Scale in Alternating Ascending and Descending 5ths

TRACK 28

Now let's take these 5ths in double stops, which is best done with fingerpicking or hybrid picking—whichever you are most comfortable with.

Pentatonic Scale in Double-Stop 5ths

TRACK 29

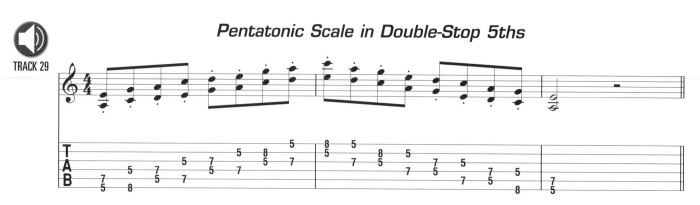

WHAMMY WIGGLIN'

I do a little whammy bar wigglin' on this next exercise so I feel the need now to give ya a few clues about keepin' your axe in tune when hittin' that thang.

It may be known to some of you that I do a ton of stuff for Fender guitars and have been doing clinics and performances for them for years. In my many travels I have been asked countless times how I keep my guitar in tune when using the whammy bar on my Strat, which does not have any kind of locking nut system on it. My initial response is "a good dose of devilry," but in actuality, I don't do much other than the following little trick when changing strings.

For some reason, a lot of guitar players make changing strings a bizarre little ritual involving the removal of all the strings at once from the instrument, the deployment of the ritualistic rag and special cleaning secretion and then a systematic de-grouting whilst chanting a mantra such as "the power of Jimi compels you, the power of Jimi compels you..." OK, the last part was a little bit of a stretch but the part about taking all the strings off at once is the dicey one when dealing with a Stratocaster with a floating bridge. "Floating bridge" refers to the bridge of the guitar being suspended off the body of the instrument by the tension of the strings countering that of the springs inside the body, allowing the user to affect the pitch, up or down, with the use of the whammy bar. A while back, after much frustration with the amount of time it was taking me to get my Strat to stay in tune after changing the strings, I began restringing by keeping the guitar in tune, removing one string, replacing it, tuning it up, yanking on it, and then retuning it until it stayed in tune. Then I would go on to the next string and repeat this process until all the strings were done. Miraculously, this allowed me to change strings scant moments before a gig and actually stay in tune. The whole process doesn't take very long and it makes a world of difference.

The primary reason guitars go out of tune when using a vibrato arm, or whammy bar as I like to call it, is because of friction on the string somewhere. That is why a little graphite on the nut and on other contact points can help keep the thing in tune when wigglin' the bar. That being said, I find that after it has been set up properly, nothing makes as big a difference in keeping the guitar in tune than changing the strings as I mentioned above. I find that the way that Fender Stratocasters come from the factory these days is exactly how I like my bridge to float. So as long as you don't change string gauges, you should be good to go. If you do change gauges, you may want to have your favorite guitar tech give it the once over with a setup.

Alrighty. Now take the double-stop 5ths exercise again, but this time add either a little whammy-bar wiggle or, like I did here, use your palm on the floating bridge and cause vibrato by applying pressure and then letting up. Listen to Track 30 and hear how this sounds, then try to replicate it.

TRACK 30

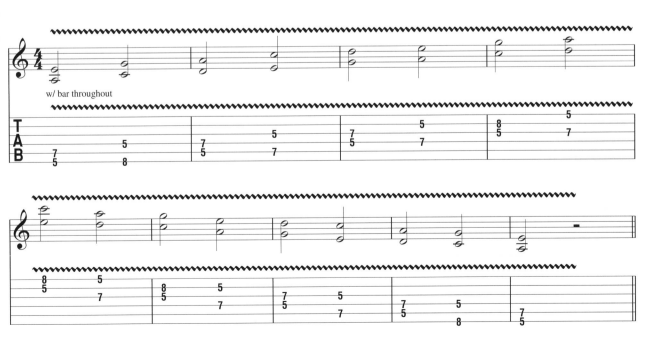

Gimme Five

Solo

This next little number deviates from our previous example improvisations by being a solo piece. It uses 5ths with some of the whammy bar vibrato that we have just discussed, along with some of the other skills honed thus far, to create a groovy little piece with an eastern flair.

When learning this piece, remember to try hybrid picking, which will be especially handy when playing the two-string trill lick in measure 4. If you don't have a whammy bar on your guitar, you can try to replicate the vibrato with your hands the "old school" way.

TRACK 31

The same clean amp setting was used as in the previous exercise with the Strat on the neck pickup.

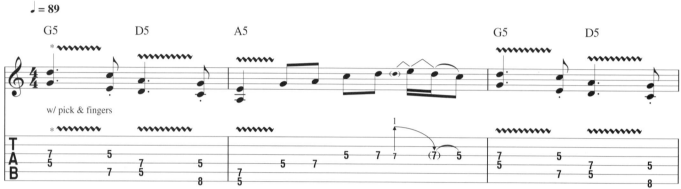

*Using a guitar with a Strat-style bridge, create vibrato by pressing and releasing bridge with palm of picking hand.

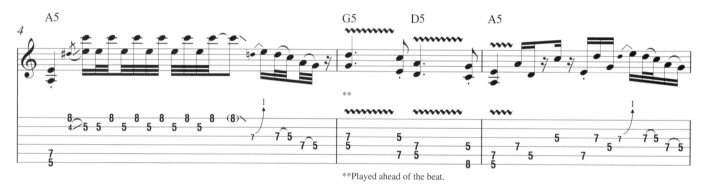

**Played ahead of the beat.

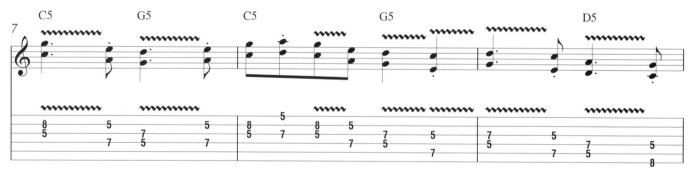

6THS AND 7THS

If we attempt to harmonize each note of the minor pentatonic scale using the intervals of 6ths or 7ths, we end up with the first note of the scale (A) being harmonized with the fifth note of the scale (G). Their relationship to each other is a minor 7th. The second scale degree (C) is harmonized with the root (A) up an octave, which is a major 6th. The third scale degree (D) is harmonized with the second (C) an octave up, which is a minor 7th. The fourth scale degree (E) is harmonized with the third scale degree (D) an octave up, which is a minor 7th, and finally, the fifth scale degree (G) with the fourth scale degree (E) an octave up, which is a major 6th.

The sound of these intervals being played is a little harder on the ear than the other intervals, but they are a cool tool nonetheless.

Check out these two exercises using 6ths and 7ths. Similar to the previous interval exercises, the first one just goes up and down the scale using the intervals, and the second one goes up one interval then down the next, which is kind of fun. These examples are played through three times each.

Pentatonic Scale in 6ths and 7ths

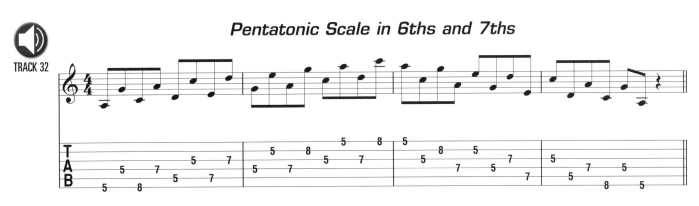

Pentatonic Scale in Alternating Ascending and Descending 6ths and 7ths

OCTAVES

These are easy enough to explain. It's just playing the same note one octave up. Just the same, it is a cool thing to have in your trick bag. The following two exercises approach octaves in the same way as our previous interval studies.

I should mention that octaves, along with 6ths and 7ths, can be played as double stops, just like we did with the 4ths and 5ths. We will allude to that in the sample improvisation "Mean Bunions."

If you want to explore the use of octaves a little more, you should get some recordings of the late, great Wes Montgomery. He developed an octave technique that the world is still trying to recover from. All of his recordings are great, but if you get the earlier recordings that he did, like *The Incredible Jazz Guitar of Wes Montgomery*, you will really get the message.

Pentatonic Scale in Octaves

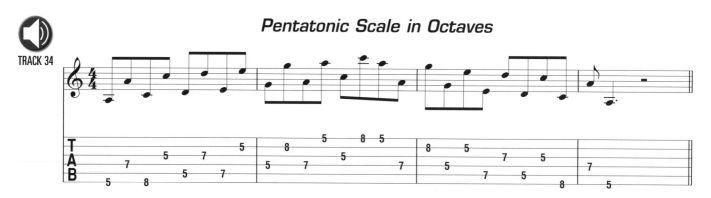

TRACK 34

Pentatonic Scale in Alternating Ascending and Descending Octaves

TRACK 35

Mean Bunions

 Lead

This next piece is a minor blues shuffle that is reminiscent of Booker T.'s "Green Onions"; hence the name "Mean Bunions," which I understand to be a dastardly foot complaint of which I have not had the displeasure.

There are lots of cool little lickeroonies in here for you to steal. Since this is the sample improvisation for the purpose of using 6th, 7th, and octave intervals in context, there are a lot of those. There are other little treats like the two opening licks, which are best achieved by using an upward sweep after the first note is played with a downstroke. It's a groovy little nuance that brings the raunch factor to the fore.

I used the same clean amp setting as the previous examples for "Mean Bunions," with the Strat on the neck pickup.

TRACK 36

Moderate Shuffle ♩ = 121

*Played
behind
the beat.

Rhythm

I think you will have fun with this little rhythm part that combines the organ part of "Green Onions" with the guitar part, and changes them up enough to keep the lawyers at bay. I'm picking this all with my fingers to give it a more organic tone. This also allows me to give the strings a little pop here and there by lifting them up slightly when plucking them. The pop happens when the strings slam back down against the frets.

TRACK 37

Moderate Shuffle ♩ = 121

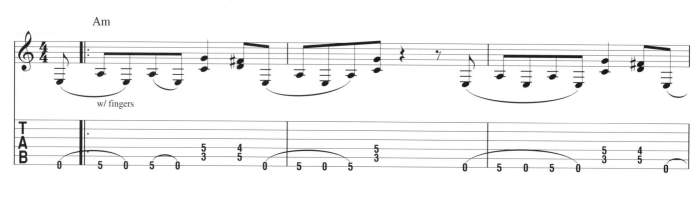

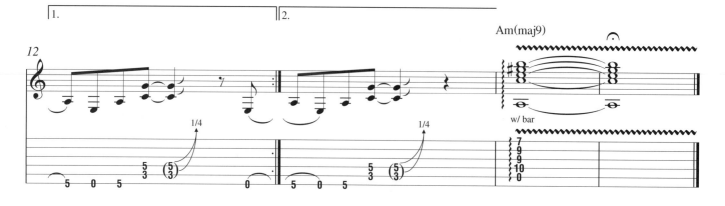

38

Mean Bunions - Rhythm

THE BLUES SCALE

The blues scale is one of the most identifiable sounds in popular music—at least in my world. I have been naughty because without saying so I have been alluding to it with bends and slides in many of the previous sample improvisation pieces. The minor pentatonic scale that we have been pummeling is made into a blues scale by adding the legendary flatted 5th—the "blue note," as it is called. The tonus diabolicus is what the medieval monks called the interval of the ♭5 when played along with the root of a scale, because they thought it sounded positively infernal and would result in unsavory activities if sounded with regularity. Judging by what I've seen, they may not have been far off the mark. But really, it's all just good, clean fun, officer.

The A Blues Scale

TRACK 38

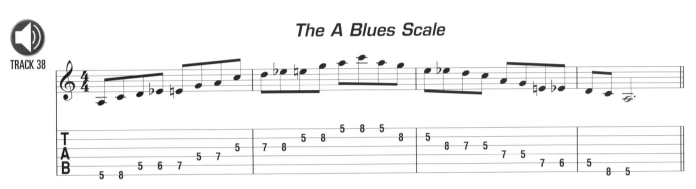

In keeping with our tradition of manipulating scales to add to our grab bag of improvisatory fodder, the next exercise breaks up the blues scale (in a way that works great with any scale, actually) by going up four notes from the root, then starting on the second note and going up four notes, and so on. Going down the scale, it works the same way. If you work this up to a frightening speed (which is not too hard), it can be a breath taker.

Blues Scale in Groups of Four

TRACK 39

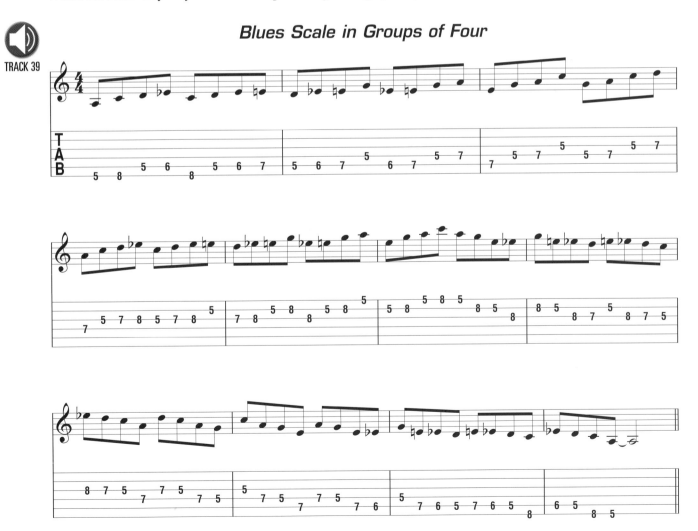

Rockin' Bloozer

Lead

I thought it would be a good idea to do a sample improvisation using the blues scale and some of the tricks we have learned thus far. I tried to jam as many speedy little blues-rock licks as possible in here for you to steal at your discretion. It is important to realize when listening to these examples that I have a tendency to use hybrid picking on all speedier licks, so if you can't get them to sound quite right and you're not hybrid picking, this could be the issue.

The first lick out of the gate here is something that I repeat a few times in "Rockin' Bloozer." I stole a variation of this lick from Dickey Betts from the Allman Brothers Band on the tune "In Memory of Elizabeth Reed." If you do not already possess the Allman Brothers' recording *Live at Fillmore East*, you need to get it because it is a veritable manifesto of blues/rock guitar savagery.

I'm just using the Blues Combo setting on my Cyber Twin SE and the bridge pickup on the ol' Strat, a Seymour Duncan JB Junior.

TRACK 40

♩ = 148

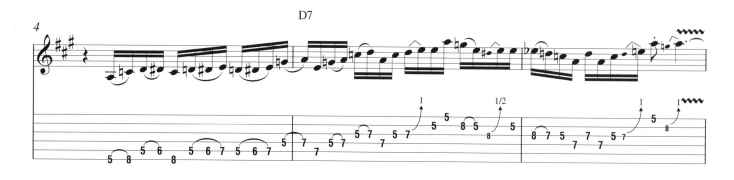

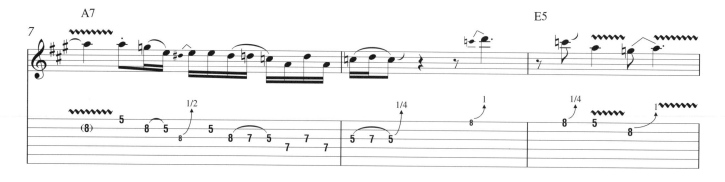

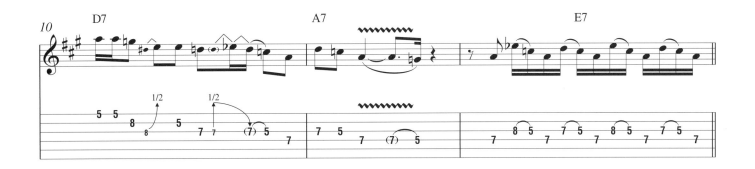

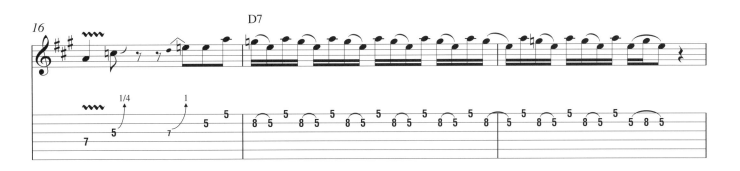

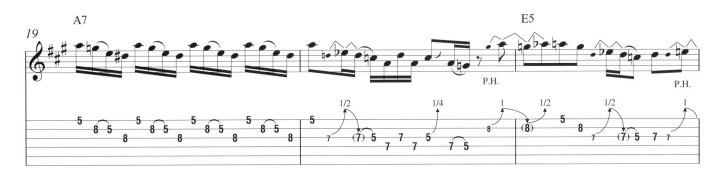

 **Rhythm**

This rhythm part is savage rock pigdom. It is a combination of Chuck Berry meets Keith Richards by way of Stevie Ray Vaughan, playing a pattern reminiscent of "Long Cool Woman." There are actually two guitars on this rhythm track so it is a little hard to discern what is going on, but I have given you the main guitar part here. This is all about attitude so don't be afraid to get sloppy and slovenly, as long as it grooves.

Muting is achieved by lightening up on the fretting hand while strumming to get that percussive effect happening. Using your pinky is a must to get the stretches up the neck. At first you will be lame if you are not used to it but—as with everything—the more you practice...

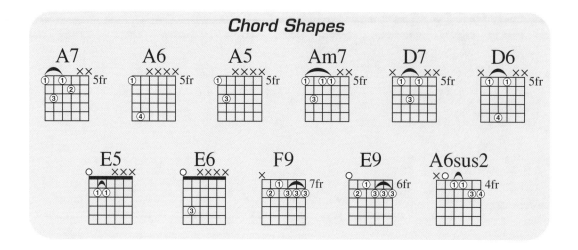

 TRACK 41

The tone here is the same clean tone we have been using with the Strat with the neck and middle pickup combination.

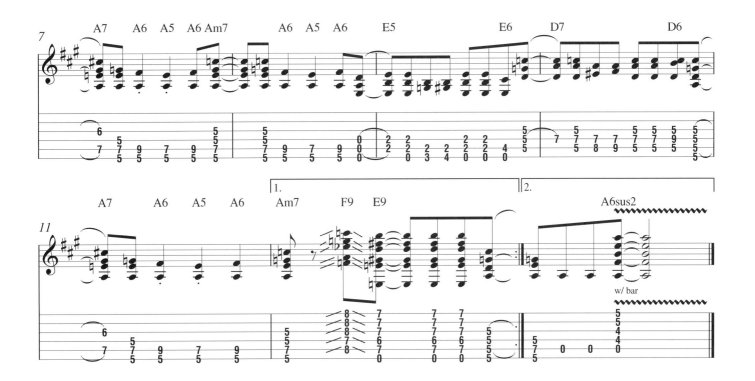

CHICKEN PICKIN'

Chicken pickin' refers to a technique and an approach to playing with deadened and popped strings that suggests the possibility of the presence of poultry in your immediate surroundings. It is most commonly affiliated with country music, although many rockers and bluesmen have used it.

I first learned chicken pickin' by listening to Dire Straits records and their illustrious leader and guitar fiend, Mark Knopfler. I then came around to all the great country guitarists via two other Englishmen named Albert Lee and Ray Flacke. It is a little strange that it would take English guitarists to turn me on to the glories of country pickin', but I grew up listening to rock 'n' roll, and a lot of it by Englishmen like the Beatles, Stones, Cream, Zeppelin, etc., so I guess it makes sense.

Albert Lee played with Eric Clapton, and the release *Just One Night* recorded in 1979 featured many a savage solo by Albert. To this day, I consider his 24-bar solo on "Further on up the Road" on that record to be one of the most perfect guitar solos of all time. It was obvious to me that there was more to his playing than just blues influences and that led me on a quest that continues to this day. First I got many of Albert's great recordings (if you can find his two instrumental records on the MCA Master Series Label—*Gagged But Not Bound* and *Speechless*—get them immediately!). Then I dug up some of his work with others, including "Luxury Liner" on the Emmylou Harris release of the same name. I found out Albert was influenced by Jimmy Bryant, James Burton, Don Rich (of Buck Owens and the Buckaroos), Cliff Gallup (of Gene Vincent and the Blue Caps), Jerry Reed, and Chet Atkins. I then got as many of those old recordings as possible and I am still working on that stuff!

Ricky Scaggs' LP *Highways and Heartaches* is a good place to start studying the Telecaster Titan, Ray Flacke. I did my best to pick this album clean of all of Ray's ramblings. My first chicken-picked note, though, occurred as a result of Mark Knopfler from Dire Straits. His clean Stratocaster tone hooked me from the get-go. The first Dire Straits LP is still my favorite, but he has done a ton of great stuff. I knew by listening to "Sultans of Swing" and "Setting Me Up" that there was something different about the way that the strings were plucked but I didn't quite know what it was until I saw a picture of Mark in a magazine. He had no pick in his hand; in fact, his picking hand looked like some kind of diabolical claw savaging the strings. I then began to experiment with this and figured it out. After a while, I realized that Albert Lee and Ray Flacke were doing the same type of thing but with hybrid picking instead of with fingers alone.

When you learn chicken pickin', you can alternate live and dead notes with extreme rapidity. It also lets you keep the string bent at the same time. There are two things that make it happen. First is the plucking of a deadened (damped) note. This a *ghost note*, which has no real pitch; it's indicated by the *x* in the notation. The tricky thing about the ghost note in this particular style is that the string-damping is done by a finger on the picking hand, not by the fretting hand, thus freeing it up for bending or sliding.

The ghost note is immediately followed by a note that is "popped." The same finger that was used to damp the string now raises it slightly, then releases it to smack the fret.

This can all be done either pickless—with your thumb and finger—or by using your pick with your middle finger, with a little bit of fingernail grabbing the string as well.

Chicken Pickin' with Thumb and Finger

First we'll try the thumb-and-finger approach. Place your picking-hand thumb on the A string, near the neck pickup. Place your first finger on the same string, a bit closer to the bridge. Pluck a note with your thumb that is thoroughly damped by the first finger. Don't be afraid to pluck with authority. After plucking this dead note, use the first finger to pull the string away from the guitar just a hair, and then release it, letting it "pop" against the frets.

Chicken Pickin' with Hybrid Picking Approach

Now let's try the hybrid-picking method. Here, you place your pick on the A string in preparation to play a downstroke, and place your middle finger near it on the same string, ready to play an upstroke. Pluck the damped note with the pick and "pop" the string immediately afterward with the **middle** finger. Try to get some fingernail into it.

Try this exercise both ways. Give Track 42 a good listen first. You'll hear the thumb-and-fingers approach at three speeds, then the hybrid-picking version at three speeds.

Chicken Pickin'

TRACK 42

Now, let's practice the two ways to chicken-pick on the blues scale. On Track 43, you'll hear this exercise played with thumb and finger at three speeds, then with pick and finger also at three speeds.

TRACK 43

Chicken Pickin' the Blues Scale

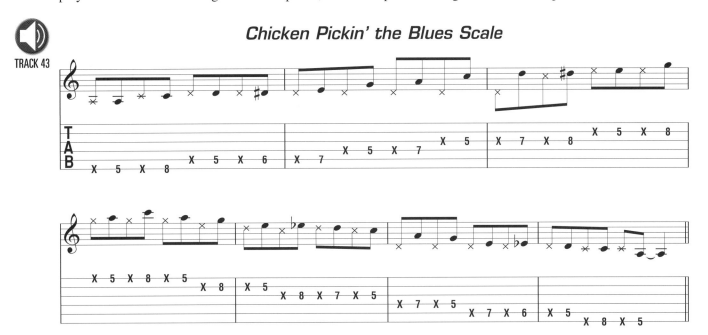

The following little rhythm snippet is another good way of practicing chicken pickin'. When I first heard Mark Knopfler doing this, I thought it was the bee's knees and had to have it. It sounds best with the thumb-and-fingers approach. You'll notice a couple of things here. First of all, you are using your thumb and first finger on the A string, so you'll have to use your middle finger when chicken-pickin' the D string, and your third finger when pickin' the G string. Second, the pattern is reversed here, so pluck the three strings first (with the first finger on the A string), followed by the damped pluck on the A string (with thumb and finger). Again, the example is played at three speeds.

TRACK 44

Chicken Pickin' Rhythm

Fowl Play

The next piece employs chicken pickin', the blues scale, and a bunch of the other stuff we've learned. This is a blues (what a surprise), and for the first two choruses, I solo using the thumb-and-finger version of chicken pickin'. For the second two choruses, I use the pick-and-finger hybrid method. For the pedal steel-type double-stop bends with chicken pickin' (a good example is in measure 25) use the pick along with the middle and ring fingers. Try starting this lick with the middle and ring fingers only, then using the pick and middle finger for the ghost note.

When we reach the V chord (E) at measure 33, we anticipate the measure with a bend from G up to A on the 2nd string. We hold this bend steady and start a repeating three-note figure. First the ring finger plucks the high C on the first string. Next, the middle finger deadens the pre-bent string 2 while the pick hits it for the ghost note. Follow up with a middle-finger pop on the same bent note. Repeat this three-note lick for two measures, clear through the D7 chord, which is the chord the lick has been anticipating all along. The A and C notes create some serious tension over the E chord, making it mighty tasty when the D7 kicks in underneath 'em.

The chicken-pickin' style doesn't always have to employ the plucking of the muted notes. It can just be that you are alternating between your thumb and finger or pick and finger to play the different notes or licks and that you pop the strings when you feel the need. Just by alternating between the fingers and thumb or pick, the tone can change. Give "Fowl Play" (Track 45) a good listen while following along with the music and get a feel for the difference in sound.

I'm not gonna lie to ya, there is some hard stuff in this one and some of it incorporates advanced hybrid picking, but fear not! You must aim high! Take your time, start off super-slow, and gradually build up the tempo on these new licks.

I switched to a Fender Custom Shop '54 Telecaster Relic Guitar for proper poultry renderings on this recording. If you are not familiar with the Relic guitars, they are "pre-distressed" to look like they have been played and pummeled for fifty-plus years. This particular guitar has medium jumbo frets, which makes bending a little easier than with the smaller vintage frets it would have had historically. It looks just like Roy Buchanan's Tele and sounds like a beast. The neck pickup is a Fender Twisted Tele, and the bridge pickup is a Fender Texas Special. I used this instrument for the remainder of the examples on the CD.

The same Fender Bassman clean amp setting as all along on the Cyber Twin SE (the "Spank That Thang" setting) was used on this track. With the volume full up on the guitar, it broke up a little bit, giving me some snarl.

TRACK 45

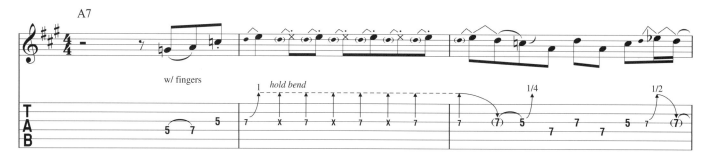

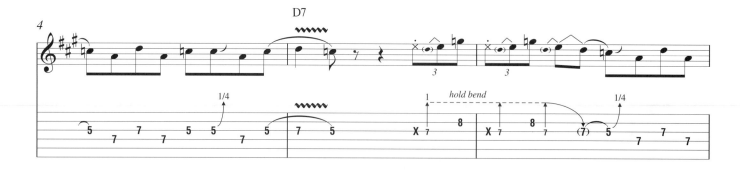

Fowl Play - Lead

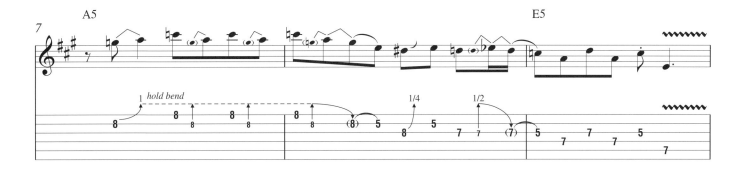

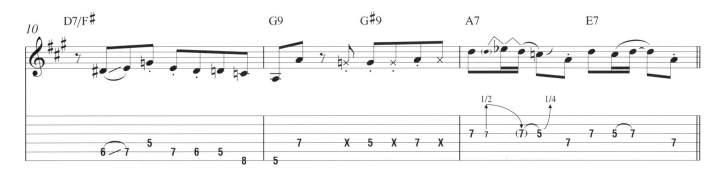

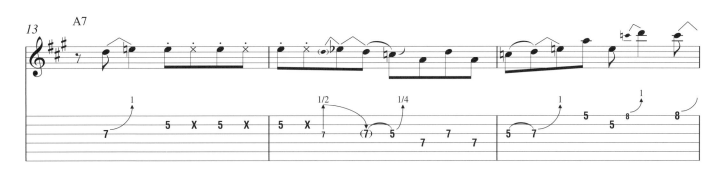

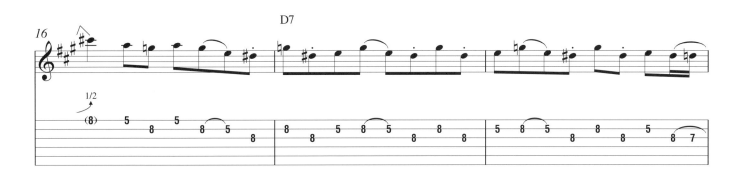

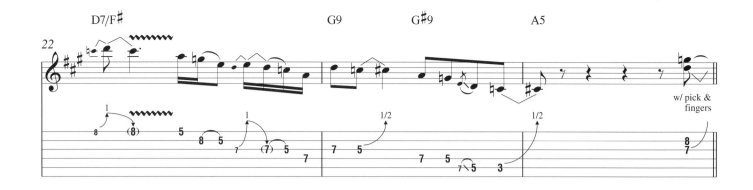

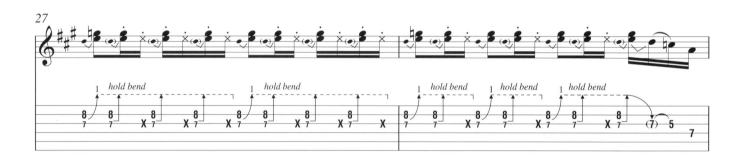

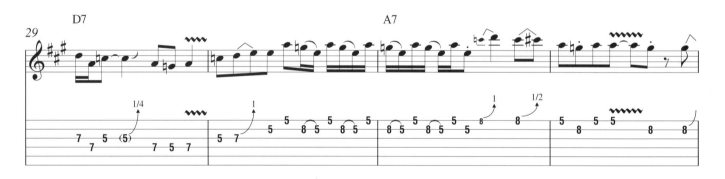

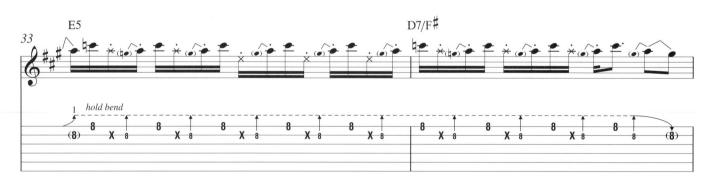

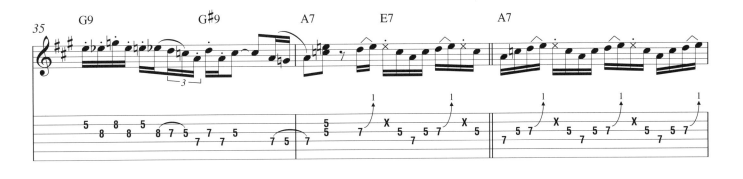

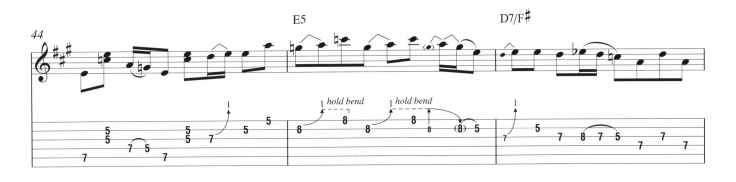

Fowl Play - Lead

Rhythm

This rhythm track takes the chicken-picked rhythm pattern that we learned earlier and turns up the funky chicken factor. Mastering this type of comping will give you a whole new slant on playing a simple Chuck Berry-ish rhythm pattern. The track is played with the thumb and first and middle fingers only. I have always felt that this approach gives a warmer tone than the hybrid method, making it better suited for this pattern—for my taste, anyway.

Notice when listening to this track that the chicken-picked note isn't always completely deadened. Sometimes it's just heavily muted to give a staccato chicken smidgeon! Variations are played on the repeats of this rhythm part, but the main pattern is given.

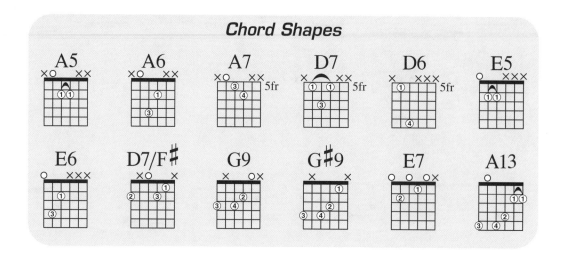

TRACK 46

♩ = 150

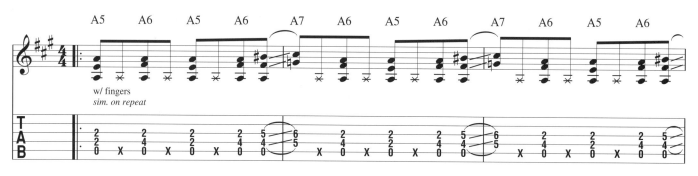

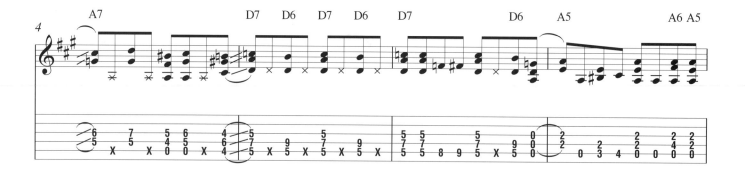

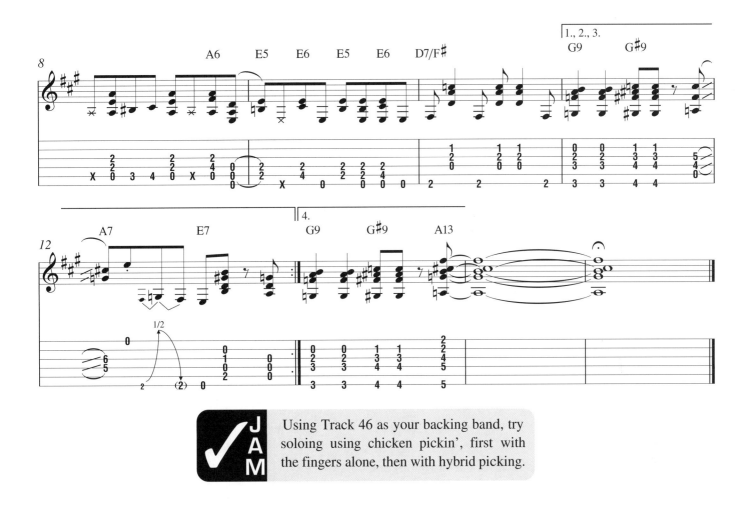

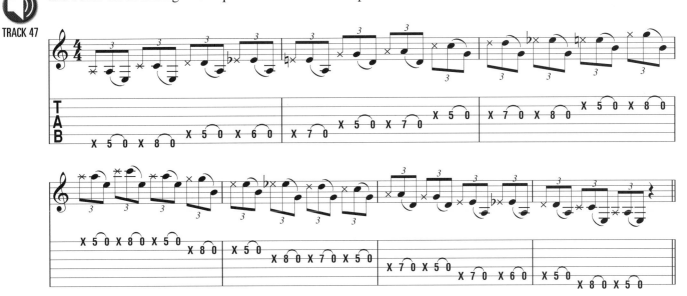

Using Track 46 as your backing band, try soloing using chicken pickin', first with the fingers alone, then with hybrid picking.

OPEN-STRING PULL-OFFS

Adding quick open-string pull-offs to licks in the chicken-pickin' style can really bump up the excitement factor. I first learned this type of playing from listening to Albert Lee's incendiary solo on Dave Edmunds's version of "Sweet Little Lisa" on *Repeat When Necessary*. He played a lick on it using an open-string pull-off that shook the foundations of my blues world! This is one of the key tools of countryesque guitarists, from Chet to Mark Knopfler to Brent Mason.

The following exercise is one of the things I always show in my clinics to give the aspiring chicken picker in the audience some tools of stylistic metamorphosis. Once the chicken-pickin' muting thang is happening with the blues scale, you can add an open-string pull-off to the mix. With just these elements, one could improvise and come off sounding like a quasi-seasoned chicken picker.

TRAVIS PICKING

Before I barrel forth and give you a sample improvisation using the open-string pull-offs, I want to show you a little Travis-picking exercise that I use on the forthcoming jam track.

Travis-picking is a fingerstyle technique. The basic approach has two main characteristics:
- The thumb or pick alternates between two bass strings on beats 1 and 3, or in steady quarter notes.
- The fingers pluck the higher strings, usually between the bass notes (on the upbeats).

The result is a driving rhythmic feel that was the backbone of the style of not only Merle Travis, but Chet Atkins and many others. If you haven't listened to Merle, at least find the tune "Cannonball Rag," and if you don't have any Chet, I recommend any of his excellent anthologies, for example *Guitar Legend: The RCA Years* or *The Essential Chet Atkins*. Although Merle and Chet used thumbpicks, this technique can also be effectively played using hybrid picking. If you add some palm muting with your picking hand on the bass notes, letting all the other notes ring, you'll achieve the sound that Merle and Chet made famous.

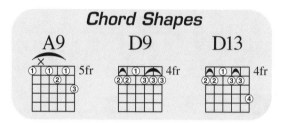

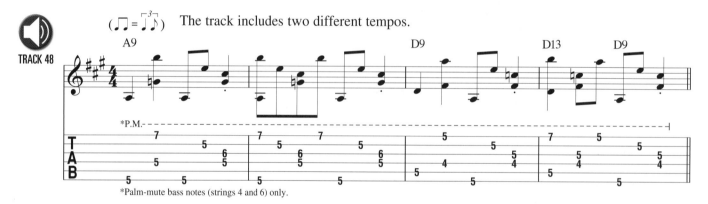

*Palm-mute bass notes (strings 4 and 6) only.

Barnyard Bonanza

Lead

This sample improvisation couples the idea of a chicken pickin', open-string pull-off-fueled lead onslaught with a Chet Atkins-like rhythm track.

The lead track here uses the blues scale and the skills we have gleaned thus far, with an exaggerated use of open-string pull-offs for you to get the idea. There is a time and a place for "less is more," but this is not one of them! The first two choruses of this blues progression were played with thumb and fingers, and the third and final chorus of the lead was done with the hybrid approach.

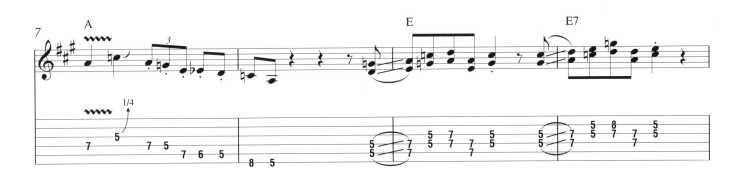

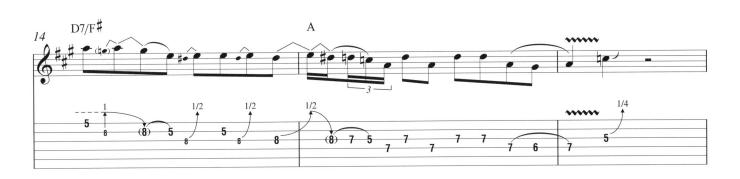

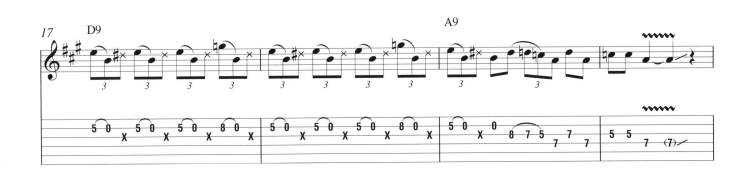

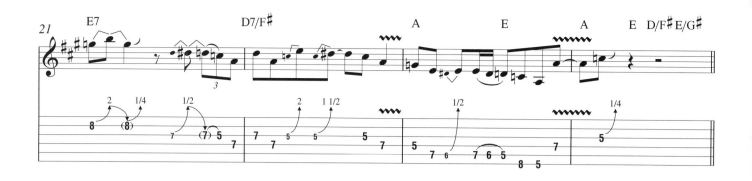

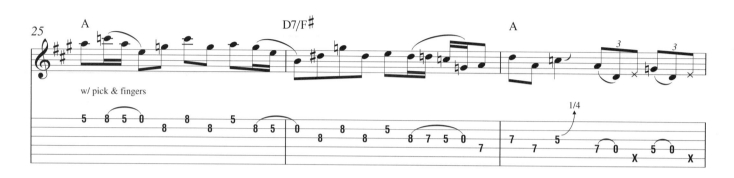

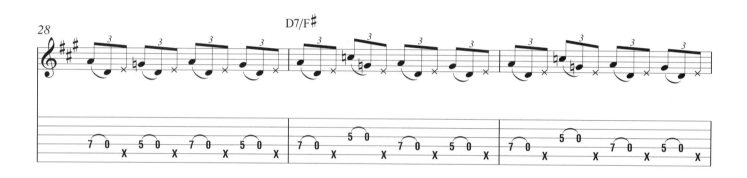

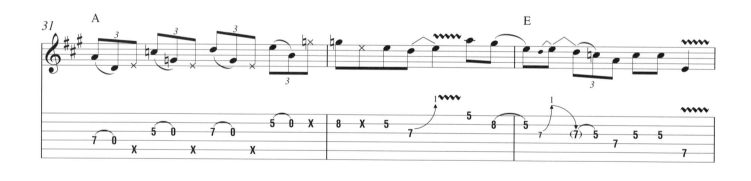

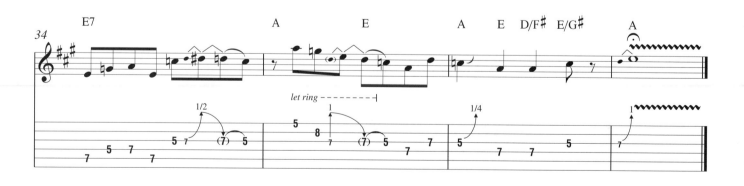

Rhythm

This rhythm track is a nod to ol' Chet, whom I feel is the greatest total guitarist I have ever had the pleasure of hearing. If only Jimi and Chet had done a record together! Using the Travis-picking tutorial given earlier as your guide, take a listen to Track 50 and then tackle this part of the rhythm track that I have transcribed for you. The second and third repeats include some variations. You can try inserting the patterns from the Track 48 example for some extra fun.

Chord Shapes

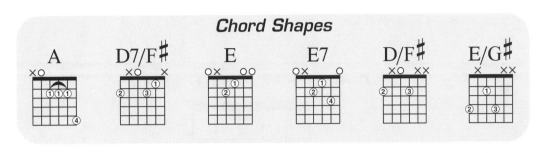

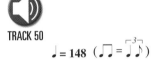

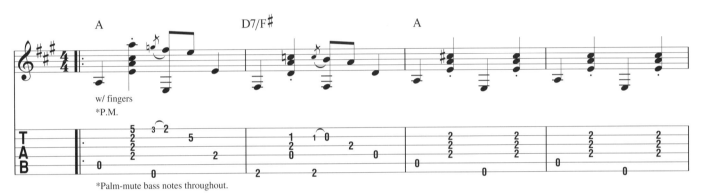

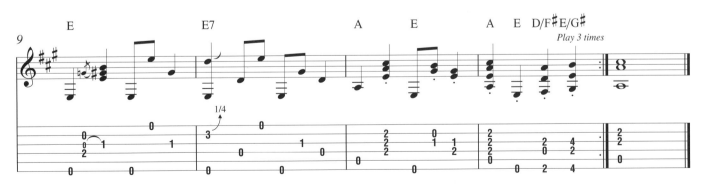

 Alright. You know what to do. Use those open string pull-offs and some chicken pickin' and wail over Track 50. Don't be afraid to let loose. When you are practicing, more is more!

MAJOR PENTATONIC SCALE

Now that we have mutilated the A minor pentatonic scale in a variety of ways (including adding the ♭5 to make it the blues scale), let's add the A major pentatonic scale to the mix.

Often at clinics I am asked what scales I use when playing over a blues, and although I throw in a lot of different flavors, including diminished and whole tone scales, I always emphasize the amount of damage one can do with just two scales: the minor pentatonic/blues scale (that we just pummeled every which way from Tuesday), and the major pentatonic scale.

A Major Pentatonic Diagram

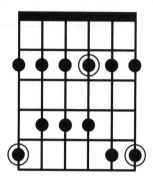

Visually, the major pentatonic scale is the same as the minor pentatonic scale, but down the neck a minor third (three frets). The root occupies a different place in the fingering pattern now. When playing minor pentatonic, the lowest root was played with your first finger at the bottom of the pattern on the 6th string. For major pentatonic, the root is the note that is played with your pinky finger on the 6th string, but the entire pattern is moved three frets down (away from the body). There are other fingering patterns, but this is the easiest.

To see how to find one position while playing the other, begin your minor pentatonic scale as we have been throughout the book, with your first finger on the 6th string at the 5th fret. Play the second note of the scale, on the 6th string at the 8th fret, with your pinky, then stop. Now slide your pinky down to where your first finger just was, at the 5th fret, and continue to use the same fingerings that you would have done in the minor pentatonic scale. You have one note available to you **below** the root on the 6th string, F♯ on the 2nd fret.

Play the A major pentatonic scale starting with your pinky on the E string at the 5th fret. Here it's played at two different tempos.

A Major Pentatonic Scale

TRACK 51

Major Pent Roundup

 **Lead**

Everything we did with the minor pentatonic scale, from bends, vibrato, and pinch harmonics, to intervallic ideas, can all be done with the major pentatonic scale. The next sample improvisation uses only the major pentatonic scale, with the tools we have learned thus far, over a four-chord vamp. There are letters placed where I allude to some of the skills we have learned up to this point, although in some cases, I did not strictly adhere to the confines of the letters.

TRACK 52

♩ = 122

A – slides	**E** – 4ths
B – bends and vibrato	**F** – 5ths
C – pinch harmonics	**G** – 6ths and 7ths
D – 2nds	**H** – octaves

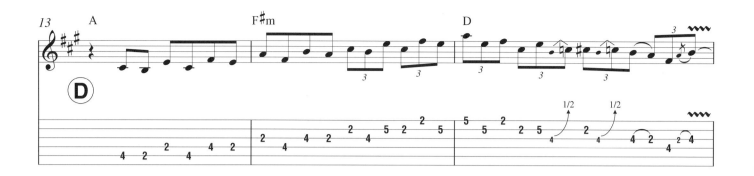

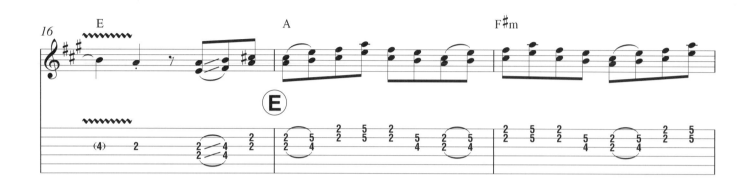

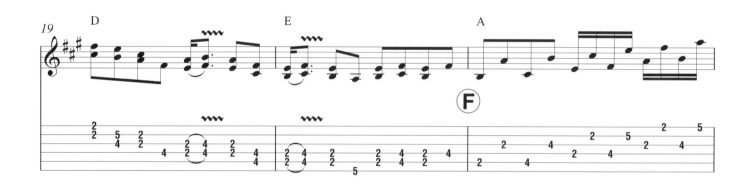

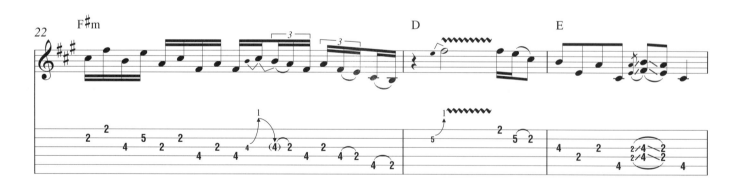

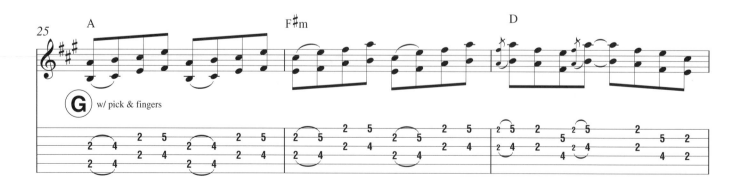

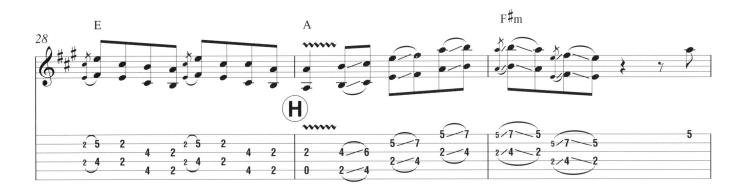

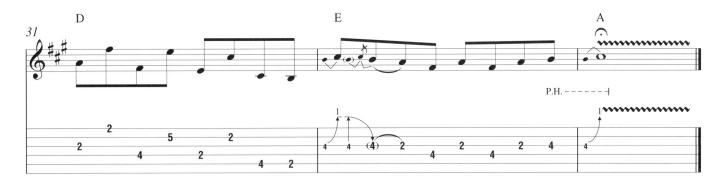

I referred to this rhythm part earlier as a four-chord *vamp*. A vamp is something that is repeated over and over—until another section is cued, for the most part. This particular vamp consists of a repeating pattern of the I, vi, IV, and V chords in the key of A major: A–F#m–D–E.

I've added little adornments to some of these chords by way of some frilly hammer-ons and whatnots for your listening and dining pleasure.

Chord Shapes

TRACK 53

♩ = 122

Using only the notes of your newly learned A major pentatonic scale and all the handy-dandy tools learned up to this point, take a stab at improvising over Track 53, "Major Pent Roundup."

MAJOR PENTATONIC SCALE WITH ADDED ♭3RD

Just like we added the ♭5th to the minor pentatonic scale to add a little flava-flave, we can add a ♭3rd to the major pentatonic scale, which, while being visually the same, produces a completely different (though instantly recognizable) sound. Here's the scale played at two different tempos.

TRACK 54

A Major Pentatonic Scale with Added ♭3rd

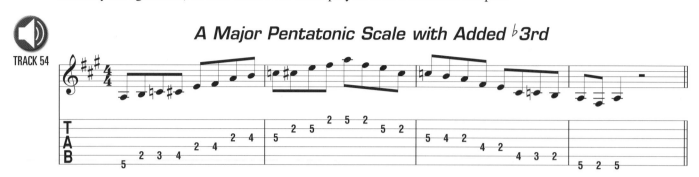

VOLUME SWELLS

Before we get into another sample improvisation, let's add some stuff to our trick bag. The volume swell is a delightful and expressive tool to have in your arsenal. Roy Buchanan was probably the first one to really define swells as an improvisational tool on the electric guitar. Lap steel and pedal-steel guitarists had previously used this technique, via a volume pedal in most cases, but Roy, and soon after, Dickey Betts on *Live at Fillmore East*, and Jeff Beck ("'Cause We've Ended as Lovers" on *Blow by Blow*) really brought them into the blues/rock world, via the volume control on the guitar itself.

This technique is easiest on a Fender Telecaster or Stratocaster due to the proximity of the volume control to the strings. Basically, you have the pinky of your picking hand on the volume control, which is rolled back so that the volume is all the way down. You then pick a note and then immediately bring the volume up. The result is a violinish tone.

Listen to Track 55 and then give this exercise a try.

TRACK 55

Volume Swell

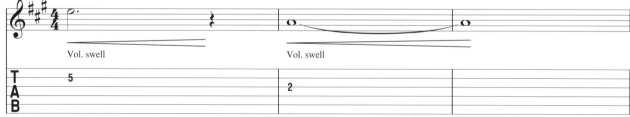

Once you get comfortable with this, you can try to speed it up a little bit. The following exercise takes our major pentatonic scale with the added ♭3rd and does the whole scale in this position using volume swells at two speeds.

TRACK 56

Volume Swell Exercise

PEDAL-STEEL EFFECT

Using the volume swell and some bending, you can approximate the sound of a pedal steel guitar. These pedal-steel licks usually incorporate bending a string while fingering another to get a unique double-stop sound.

The late Clarence White from the country-flavored rock band the Byrds helped develop a device for his Telecaster called a B-Bender. This device raises the B string up a whole step (usually) so that you can apply precise bends to a note within a chord or double stop, like a pedal steel guitar. Jimmy Page also championed the B-Bender on the Zeppelin record *In Through the Out Door* and with his 1980s aggregation called the Firm. The B-Bender is activated by pulling down the neck slightly, which brings the strap button closest to the neck up, thereby raising the pitch via an elaborate series of springs and levers inside the guitar body.

Another implement called the Hipshot raises the pitch of the B string via a bar that hangs down off the guitar next to your hip that you apply pressure to. Will Ray from the Tele-mauling Hellecasters has mastered this approach.

Having described all these gadgets, let me say you can sound like a pedal steel guitar with your bare hands as well!

Check out this exercise. With the volume turned down, pluck the two notes of a double-stop. Then turn the volume up as you bend the lower note. Also practice it the other way: with the volume down, pre-bend the lower note and pluck both strings. Just as you turn the volume up (or a little later) release the bent string.

Pedal Steel Exercise

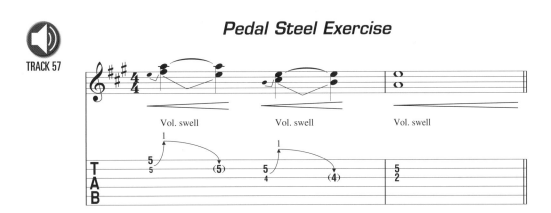

TRACK 57

Steelin' Swells

As you might guess from the title of this tune, it has a healthy dose of volume swells and pedal-steel licks. Some of these bends and vibratos are not easy but by giving the track a good listen, you should be able to approximate them.

I am using the notes of the A major pentatonic scale, but sometimes I throw in the major 7th (G#) which is not in the pentatonic scale. What can I say? I couldn't resist. And it's not really naughty, because this note is found in the complete major scale, of which major pentatonic can be considered a subset.

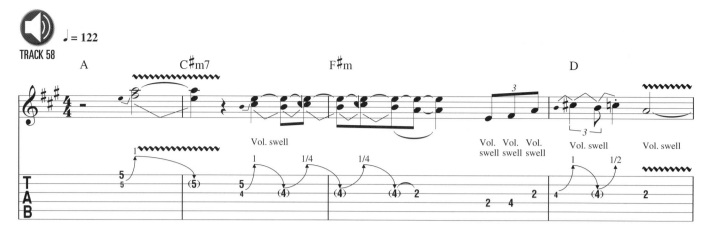

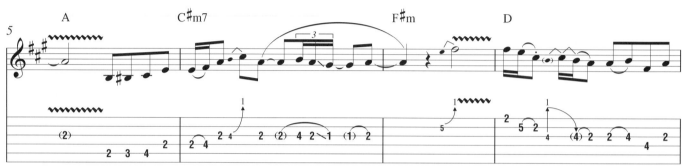

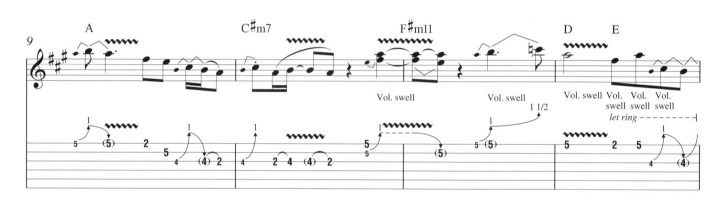

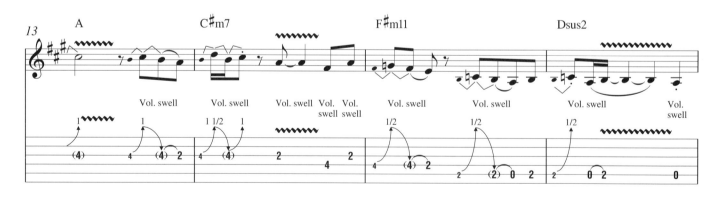

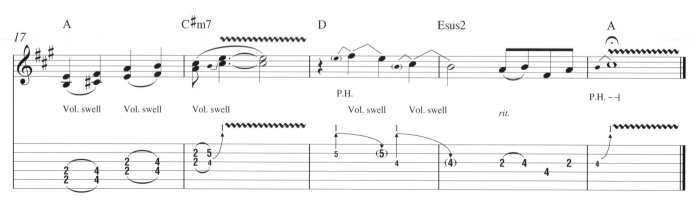

Steelin' Swells - Lead

Rhythm

This rhythm part is another nod to Jimi. Could anything be more twisted than pedal steel licks being played over a Jimi-esque rhythm part? I aim to disturb. There are a lot of double-stop rhythmic salvos that are reminiscent of Jimi's tune "Axis: Bold as Love," an anthemic jam of epic proportions. Here are the basic chord shapes used in this rhythm part. You'll notice I add in the occasional V chord or sus chord on the repeat.

Now comes the glorious time for you to employ the volume swells, pedal-steel bends and major pentatonic scale with the added flatted 3rd, and unleash a savage improvisatory barrage over Track 59.

Intersection Blues

Lead

If you are soloing over a blues that uses dominant 7th chords, or basically any basic blues that is not a minor blues, you can use a combination of the minor pentatonic scale with the added flatted 5th (blues scale) and the major pentatonic scale with the added flatted 3rd (the redneck scale! Just kidding; how about calling it a "country blues scale?"). In other words, you can "intersect" these scales—get it?

I do a lot of playing of an idea in one scale and then doing the same idea in the other scale to show you how they work together yet sound different.

There's a snazzy little harmonic lick at the tail end of this track where you have to bend the B string up a whole step *behind* the nut, using your third finger (and first and second fingers for added strength) of your fretting hand. This works best on a Tele or a Strat, and is a painful experience at first, but anything worthwhile is!

I start out on the neck pickup on the Telecaster and switch to the bridge pickup to make the pedal steel bends and the pinch harmonics sing a little more. The amp setting is still the Bassman.

Listen to "Intersection Blues" and feel the power of these two scales working together and then steal some or all of it, depending on how you like to roll.

TRACK 60

♩ = 122

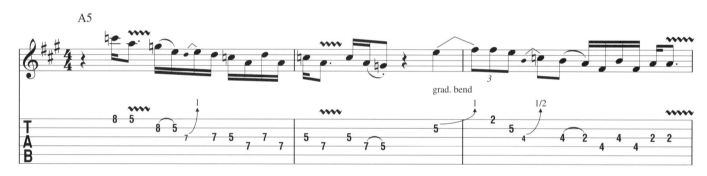

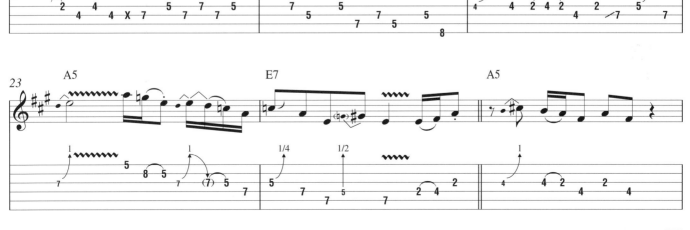

Intersection Blues - Lead

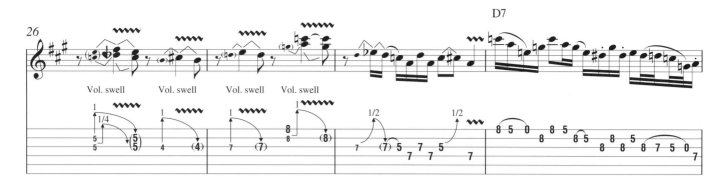

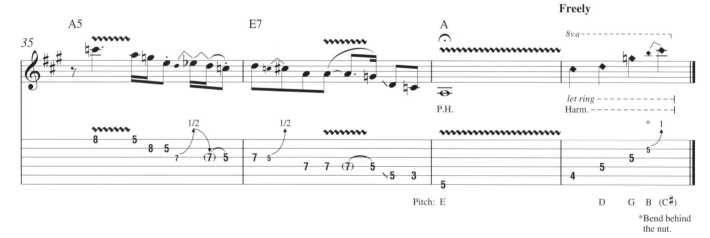

This rhythm part is kind of a chicken-pickin' version of Cream's rendition of "Crossroads" or "For the Love of a Woman" by Albert King, but not quite. Lawyers can stand down, as all is fair in love and blues riffs—to a point.

Anyway, lose the pick and try playing the rhythm pattern to "Intersection Blues." The repeats include some variations as usual.

BLUES SCALE AND MAJOR PENTATONIC EXTENSIONS

As you may have noticed, I have been trying to get you to make the most out of the smallest amount of notes and sticking to two positions that visually are exactly the same. I could easily just give you a diagram of these scales all over the neck at this point and wrap this book up. However, I have decided to give you just one more tidbit of both scales that is easily identifiable and that can be put to use immediately without your brain undergoing severe strain. I'm not questioning your intelligence. I just know from experience that most people perceive the neck of the guitar as a deep abyss whose mysteries only reveal themselves in small degrees.

Here is an extension of our A blues scale played at three tempos that you can easily slide up from, or back down to, our original position.

Blues Scale Extension

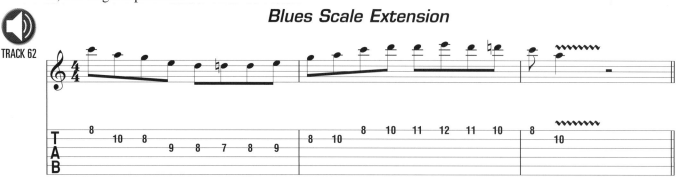

TRACK 62

Here is the same extension as it applies to our major pentatonic scale with added ♭3rd.

Country Blues Scale Extension

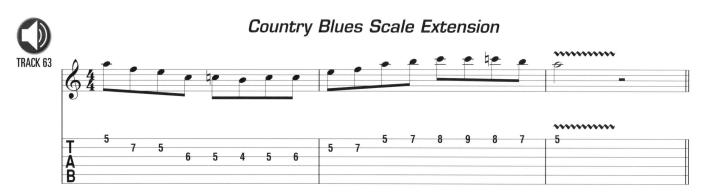

TRACK 63

Bring It

The final improvisation uses many of the ideas we've studied and gives special attention to our scale extensions. As you may have noticed, the scale extensions make the scales overlap here and there, which gives you the power to draw from the notes of both scales in the same position, adding to your tonal palette.

You can do the same things with the extensions that we have done to the other scale positions in regard to bends, vibrato, scalar manipulation, etc. After a while, you begin to find zones where things work better than in others and you start to develop your own way of doing things.

As you listen to "Bring It," you'll notice that for the first twelve bars, I stick to primarily the blues scale extension with a little overlap here and there. For the second twelve bars, I try to stick to the major pentatonic extension, and from there I mix it up. At some points I add chromatic notes in to add a little flavor, like adding mortar between the bricks. Don't be alarmed; if it feels good, do it!

I'm using the Tele still; I start out on the neck pickup, and as the solo builds, I switch to the bridge pickup for a little more growl. The amp setting is the same: sweet Bassman—via Cyber Twin SE, that is.

 Listen to "Bring It" while following along with the music and then begin with the decimation.

TRACK 64

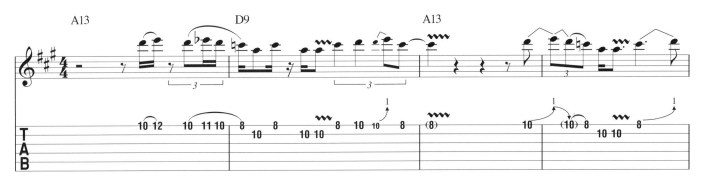

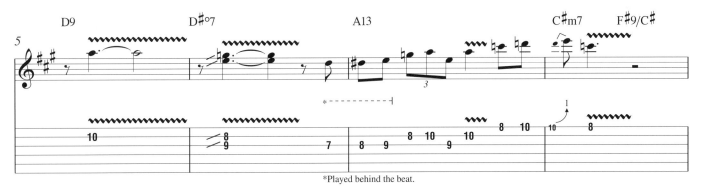

*Played behind the beat.

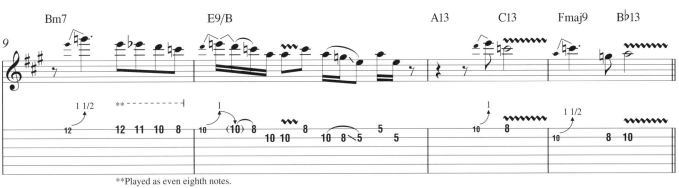

**Played as even eighth notes.

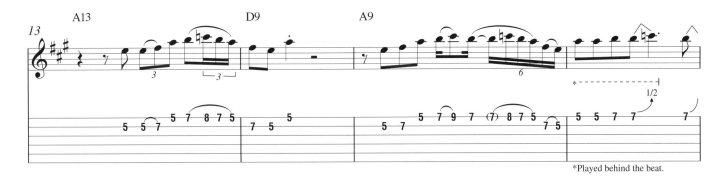

*Played behind the beat.

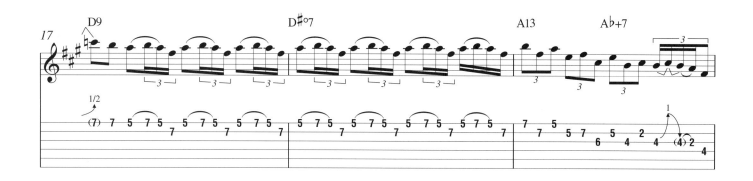

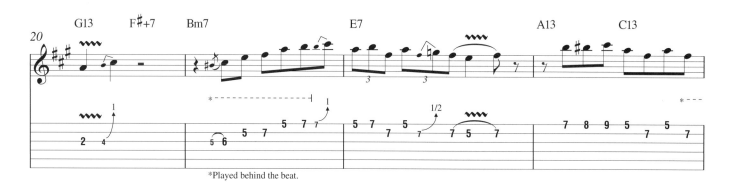

*Played behind the beat.

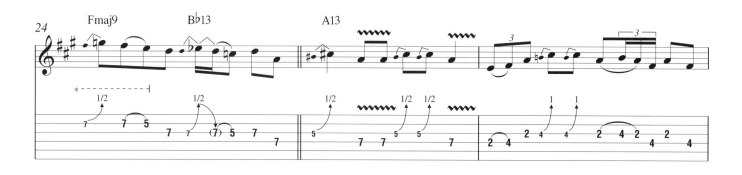

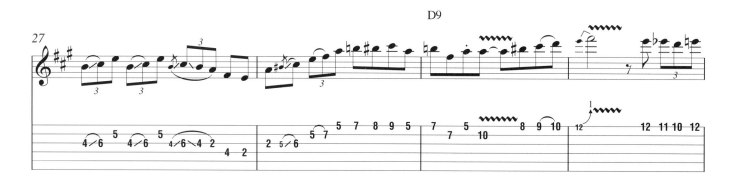

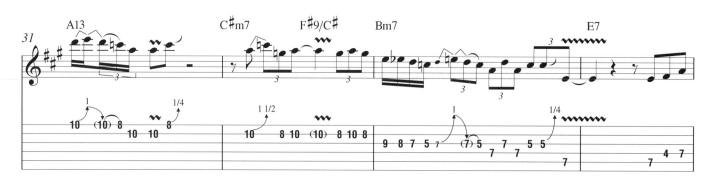

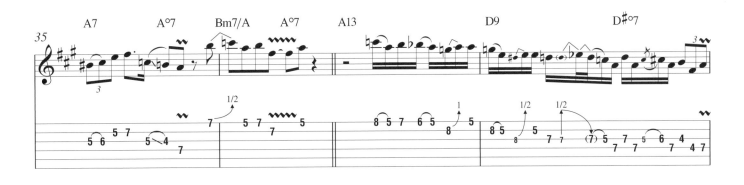

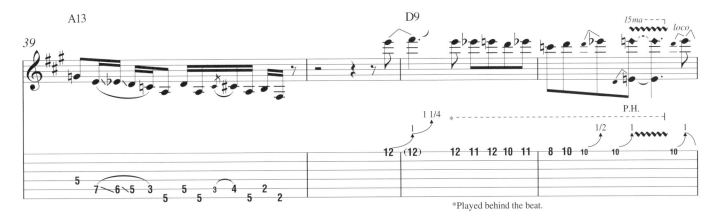

*Played behind the beat.

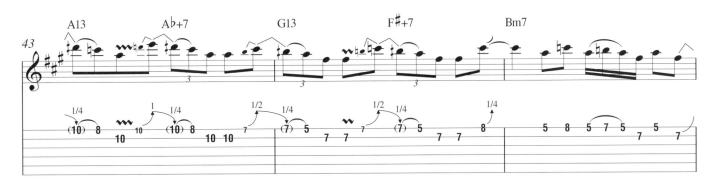

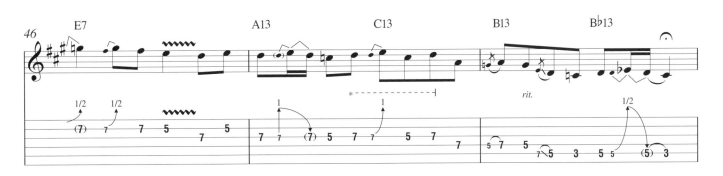

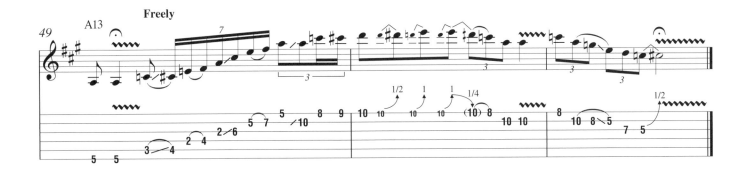

 **Rhythm**

I added the Vibratone effect to the Bassman setting on my amp to get an organ-like tone. The Vibratone was Fender's version of a rotating speaker like organ players use to get that delicious vibrato-y sound. Fender has recreated it convincingly within the Cyber Twin SE.

Another one of my favorite guitar players, Danny Gatton, used a rotating speaker to get an organ-like tone. If you don't have any of Danny's records, all of his releases are great, but *Unfinished Business* is probably my favorite. Danny was another player I would describe as the best of the best.

On the rhythm part to "Bring It," I am emulating an organ part that incorporates the bass notes as well as the chords. Many great jazz guitarists like Joe Pass could play solo guitar pieces that combined a walking bass line with chords. A fella named Lenny Breau would play the bass line, chords, and leads at the same time. These people were freaks who apparently had nothing better to do than practice all day to develop techniques to humiliate and confound their fellow guitarists! Their renderings are utterly delightful!

I tried to come up with a part that conjured up the feel of an organ, but that was also not too difficult. Using your fingers with thumb is going to work best here.

Listen to Track 65. I have transcribed the first twenty-four bars—the rest is a variation of this. Practice slowly, sometimes breaking things down measure by measure to work on the coordination. Remember, the metronome is your friend. Set it only as fast as you can play the piece error-free.

Chord Shapes

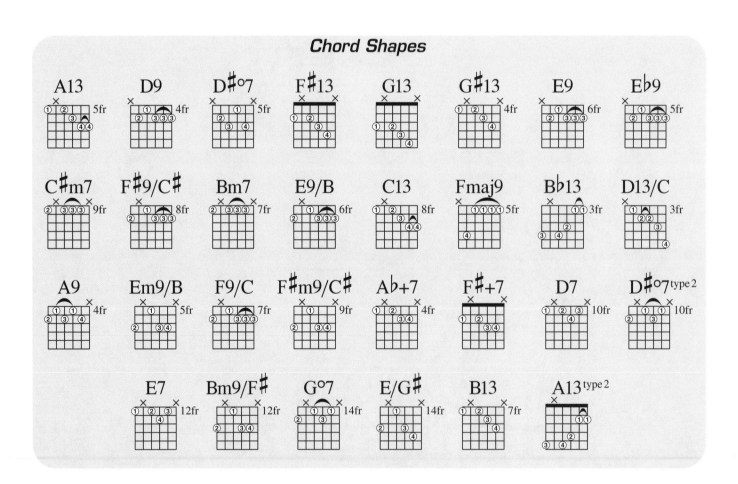

Give it a try!

It is time for our last jam. Use all the tools you have learned and unleash. Try using just one scale and then the other and then try mixing it up. Try taking just a couple of the tools we have learned, and milking them for all they are worth. Whatever ya do, have fun!

Bring It - Rhythm

BLUES JAM ETIQUETTE

Playing with other live human beings is the best way to get your timing together, to learn to develop solos, to get an understanding of dynamics, to get a tone happening, and so on. If getting your own band together to either rehearse and/or perform is not practical at the moment, going to a blues jam at a local club is not a bad idea. It is important, however, to be familiar with some of the rules of engagement to avoid an unpleasant experience (although some are seemingly unavoidable, but do not let that deter you!).

First of all, make certain that it is an "open jam" before bringing in your guitar and stating a desire to sit in. Going into a club, no matter how unassuming it may seem, and asking to sit in with a random band on a random night is a recipe for disaster. It may be no big deal, or it may be like asking some stranger to let you dance with his wife. Why chance it?

Once the jam has been sussed, be apprised that the band leader hosting the jam can range from 1) a benevolent soul who enjoys playing with other musicians so much that he has decided to provide an opportunity to jam with friends and to nurture fledgling instrumentalists on an off night for a nominal fee to 2) a bitter bar-band grifter who wants to enjoy another evening of free drinks and the opportunity to humiliate lesser-qualified musicians over endless renditions of tunes like "Sweet Home Chicago" and "Mustang Sally." Sometimes these two descriptions can apply to the same individual from one week to the next! So, beware!

Inform the leader of the jam of your desire to sit in. Do not give him your history up to that point, your favorite bands or nostril circumference. If you have a mutual acquaintance that is genuine, mention it and this may save you the trouble of waiting for three hours to play. Other than that, he or she will probably ask you if you can sing. If you can, it means they can take a break and go to the bar, so the likelihood of you getting up sooner than later is good. If you don't sing, grab a seat because it could be a while, and lay low on the sauce. A drunken musician is about as *en vogue* as a leisure suit.

When you finally get up to jam, make sure you are in tune, and it is helpful if you have your own guitar cord. Most jams have amps ready to go and some folks get a little weird if you walk in with your own amp, but keep one in the trunk just in case.

One of the members of the house band will probably be up there with you but sometimes they will just call up people on the different instruments and let you figure it out from there. Whoever is singing will shout out "this is a shuffle in A" or "slow one in E from the V," or else they will just blast off, and you are expected to hang on for dear life.

Whatever you do, be sensitive even if the others are barbarians. Watch your volume, be attentive for cues and listen, listen, listen. When given a solo, the unwritten law is to take two choruses or twenty-four bars. You may be egged on to do more, or they may cut you off after one chorus. Watch and listen.

The other unwritten rule is to play two tunes and get off. Some may stay longer because they are friends of the band or whatever, but two tunes is usually the norm.

After a few of these jams you will have sussed out the posers from the folks who just want to play and get better, and you may even find potential band mates. If you use the above as a warning, if anything, you should be able to weather the phenomenon that is the blues jam.

Thanks folks, and stay tuned for more Guitar Clues!

ABOUT THE AUTHOR

Greg Koch – Internationally-renowned recording artist and guitarist, session player, author, magazine columnist, radio personality, and one of the most in-demand guitar clinicians in the world for Fender Musical Instruments and the Hal Leonard Corporation.

Visit him online at *gregkoch.com*.

Check out these other great Hal Leonard products from Greg Koch:

Book/CD packs:
Hal Leonard Guitar Method Book 1 (HL00699027)
Hal Leonard Guitar Method Book 2 (HL00697313)
Hal Leonard Guitar Method Book 3 (HL00697316)
Hal Leonard Guitar Method Complete Edition – Books 1, 2, & 3 (HL00697342)
Hal Leonard Blues Guitar Method (HL00697326)
Hal Leonard Country Guitar Method (HL00697337)
Hal Leonard Lead Licks Guitar Method (HL00697345)
Hal Leonard Rhythm Riffs Guitar Method (HL00697346)
Greg Koch Guitar Play-Along (HL00699646)

DVDs:
Guitar Gristle (HL00320376)
Stevie Ray Vaughan Greatest Hits Guitar Signature Licks (HL00320256)
Best of Stevie Ray Vaughan Guitar Signature Licks (HL00320257)

GUITAR NOTATION LEGEND

Guitar music can be notated three different ways: on a *musical staff*, in *tablature*, and in *rhythm slashes*.

RHYTHM SLASHES are written above the staff. Strum chords in the rhythm indicated. Use the chord diagrams found at the top of the first page of the transcription for the appropriate chord voicings. Round noteheads indicate single notes.

THE MUSICAL STAFF shows pitches and rhythms and is divided by bar lines into measures. Pitches are named after the first seven letters of the alphabet.

TABLATURE graphically represents the guitar fingerboard. Each horizontal line represents a string, and each number represents a fret.

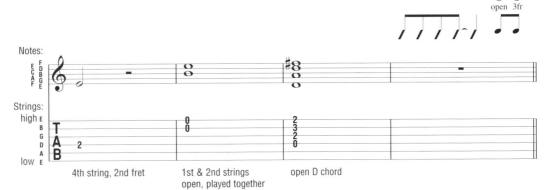

4th string, 2nd fret   1st & 2nd strings open, played together   open D chord

DEFINITIONS FOR SPECIAL GUITAR NOTATION

HALF-STEP BEND: Strike the note and bend up 1/2 step.

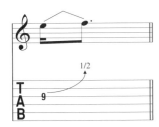

WHOLE-STEP BEND: Strike the note and bend up one step.

GRACE NOTE BEND: Strike the note and immediately bend up as indicated.

SLIGHT (MICROTONE) BEND: Strike the note and bend up 1/4 step.

BEND AND RELEASE: Strike the note and bend up as indicated, then release back to the original note. Only the first note is struck.

PRE-BEND: Bend the note as indicated, then strike it.

PRE-BEND AND RELEASE: Bend the note as indicated. Strike it and release the bend back to the original note.

UNISON BEND: Strike the two notes simultaneously and bend the lower note up to the pitch of the higher.

VIBRATO: The string is vibrated by rapidly bending and releasing the note with the fretting hand.

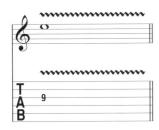

WIDE VIBRATO: The pitch is varied to a greater degree by vibrating with the fretting hand.

HAMMER-ON: Strike the first (lower) note with one finger, then sound the higher note (on the same string) with another finger by fretting it without picking.

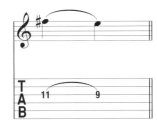

PULL-OFF: Place both fingers on the notes to be sounded. Strike the first note and without picking, pull the finger off to sound the second (lower) note.

LEGATO SLIDE: Strike the first note and then slide the same fret-hand finger up or down to the second note. The second note is not struck.

SHIFT SLIDE: Same as legato slide, except the second note is struck.

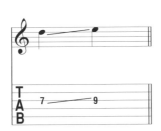

TRILL: Very rapidly alternate between the notes indicated by continuously hammering on and pulling off.

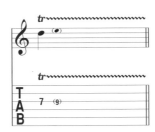

TAPPING: Hammer ("tap") the fret indicated with the pick-hand index or middle finger and pull off to the note fretted by the fret hand.

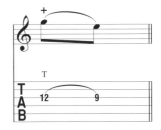

NATURAL HARMONIC: Strike the note while the fret-hand lightly touches the string directly over the fret indicated.

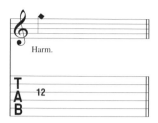

PINCH HARMONIC: The note is fretted normally and a harmonic is produced by adding the edge of the thumb or the tip of the index finger of the pick hand to the normal pick attack.

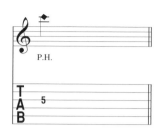

HARP HARMONIC: The note is fretted normally and a harmonic is produced by gently resting the pick hand's index finger directly above the indicated fret (in parentheses) while the pick hand's thumb or pick assists by plucking the appropriate string.

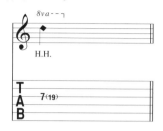

PICK SCRAPE: The edge of the pick is rubbed down (or up) the string, producing a scratchy sound.

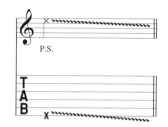

MUFFLED STRINGS: A percussive sound is produced by laying the fret hand across the string(s) without depressing, and striking them with the pick hand.

PALM MUTING: The note is partially muted by the pick hand lightly touching the string(s) just before the bridge.

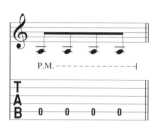

RAKE: Drag the pick across the strings indicated with a single motion.

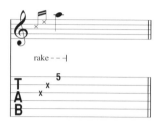

TREMOLO PICKING: The note is picked as rapidly and continuously as possible.

ARPEGGIATE: Play the notes of the chord indicated by quickly rolling them from bottom to top.

VIBRATO BAR DIVE AND RETURN: The pitch of the note or chord is dropped a specified number of steps (in rhythm), then returned to the original pitch.

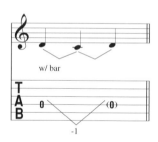

VIBRATO BAR SCOOP: Depress the bar just before striking the note, then quickly release the bar.

VIBRATO BAR DIP: Strike the note and then immediately drop a specified number of steps, then release back to the original pitch.

ADDITIONAL MUSICAL DEFINITIONS

(accent)	•	Accentuate note (play it louder).
(accent)	•	Accentuate note with great intensity.
(staccato)	•	Play the note short.
	•	Downstroke
V	•	Upstroke
D.S. al Coda	•	Go back to the sign (𝄋), then play until the measure marked "*To Coda*," then skip to the section labelled "**Coda**."
D.C. al Fine	•	Go back to the beginning of the song and play until the measure marked "*Fine*" (end).

Rhy. Fig. • Label used to recall a recurring accompaniment pattern (usually chordal).

Riff • Label used to recall composed, melodic lines (usually single notes) which recur.

Fill • Label used to identify a brief melodic figure which is to be inserted into the arrangement.

Rhy. Fill • A chordal version of a Fill.

tacet • Instrument is silent (drops out).

• Repeat measures between signs.

• When a repeated section has different endings, play the first ending only the first time and the second ending only the second time.

NOTE: Tablature numbers in parentheses mean:
1. The note is being sustained over a system (note in standard notation is tied), or
2. The note is sustained, but a new articulation (such as a hammer-on, pull-off, slide or vibrato) begins, or
3. The note is a barely audible "ghost" note (note in standard notation is also in parentheses).

Get Better at Guitar

...with these Great Guitar Instruction Books from Hal Leonard!

101 GUITAR TIPS
INCLUDES TAB

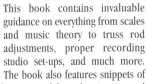

STUFF ALL THE PROS KNOW AND USE
by Adam St. James

This book contains invaluable guidance on everything from scales and music theory to truss rod adjustments, proper recording studio set-ups, and much more. The book also features snippets of advice from some of the most celebrated guitarists and producers in the music business, including B.B. King, Steve Vai, Joe Satriani, Warren Haynes, Laurence Juber, Pete Anderson, Tom Dowd and others, culled from the author's hundreds of interviews.

00695737 Book/CD Pack...$16.95

AMAZING PHRASING
INCLUDES TAB

50 WAYS TO IMPROVE YOUR IMPROVISATIONAL SKILLS
by Tom Kolb

This book/CD pack explores all the main components necessary for crafting well-balanced rhythmic and melodic phrases. It also explains how these phrases are put together to form cohesive solos. Many styles are covered – rock, blues, jazz, fusion, country, Latin, funk and more – and all of the concepts are backed up with musical examples. The companion CD contains 89 demos for listening, and most tracks feature full-band backing.

00695583 Book/CD Pack...$17.95

BLUES YOU CAN USE
INCLUDES TAB

by John Ganapes

A comprehensive source designed to help guitarists develop both lead and rhythm playing. Covers: Texas, Delta, R&B, early rock and roll, gospel, blues/rock and more. Includes: 21 complete solos • chord progressions and riffs • turnarounds • moveable scales and more. CD features leads and full band backing.

00695007 Book/CD Pack...$19.95

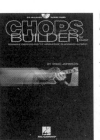

CHOPS BUILDER
INCLUDES TAB

TECHNIQUE EXERCISES FOR THE INTERMEDIATE TO ADVANCED GUITARIST
by Chad Johnson

Topics covered in this book/CD pack include: alternate picking, economy picking, sweep picking, fingerstyle, chicken pickin', classical, legato, tapping and more. Each technique is isolated, then applied to a range of musical styles.

00697339 Book/CD Pack...$14.95

FRETBOARD ROADMAPS
by Fred Sokolow

Learn how to play lead and rhythm anywhere on the fretboard, in any key; play a variety of lead guitar styles; play chords and progressions anywhere on the fretboard; expand your chord vocabulary; and think the way the pros do. Absolute beginners can follow the diagrams and instruction, and intermediate and advanced players can use the chapters non-sequentially to increase their understanding of the guitar.

00696514 ....$9.95

THE GUITAR F/X COOKBOOK
INCLUDES TAB

by Chris Amelar

The ultimate source for guitar tricks, effects, and other unorthodox techniques. This book demonstrates and explains 45 incredible guitar sounds using common stomp boxes and a few unique techniques, including: pick scraping, police siren, ghost slide, church bell, jaw harp, delay swells, looping, monkey's scream, cat's meow, race car, pickup tapping, and much more.

00695080 Book/CD Pack...$14.95

GUITAR TECHNIQUES
INCLUDES TAB

by Michael Mueller

Guitar Techniques is a terrific reference and teaching companion, as it clearly defines and demonstrates how to properly execute cool moves ranging from bending, vibrato and legato to tapping, whammy bar and playing with your teeth! The CD contains 92 demonstration tracks in country, rock, pop and jazz styles. Essential techniques covered include: fretting • strumming • trills • picking • vibrato • tapping • bends • harmonics • muting • slides • and more.

00695562 Book/CD Pack...$14.95

INTRODUCTION TO GUITAR TONE & EFFECTS

by David M. Brewster

This book/CD pack teaches the basics of guitar tones and effects, with audio examples on CD. Readers will learn about: overdrive, distortion and fuzz • using equalizers • modulation effects • reverb and delay • multi-effect processors • and more.

00695766 Book/CD Pack...$14.95

PICTURE CHORD ENCYCLOPEDIA

This comprehensive guitar chord resource for all playing styles and levels features five voicings of 44 chord qualities for all twelve keys – 2,640 chords in all! For each, there is a clearly illustrated chord frame, as well as *an actual photo* of the chord being played! Includes info on basic fingering principles, open chords and barre chords, partial chords and broken-set forms, and more.

00695224 ....$19.95

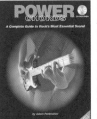

POWER CHORDS
INCLUDES TAB

A COMPLETE GUIDE TO ROCK'S MOST ESSENTIAL SOUND
by Adam Perlmutter

Learn to master rock's most tried-and-true sound: the power chord. With just a few different power chord shapes, you can rock through hundreds of songs – from death metal, to rockabilly, to grunge and beyond. This book/CD pack includes: famous progressions from popular songs, by artists from Alice in Chains to Weezer • clear photos and frames of all the essential power chords • riffs in all styles • alternate tunings • notes and tab.

00695745 Book/CD Pack...$14.95

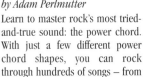

SCALE CHORD RELATIONSHIPS
INCLUDES TAB

by Michael Mueller & Jeff Schroedl

This book teaches players how to determine which scales to play with which chords, so guitarists will never have to fear chord changes again! This book/CD pack explains how to: recognize keys • analyze chord progressions • use the modes • play over nondiatonic harmony • use harmonic and melodic minor scales • use symmetrical scales such as chromatic, whole-tone and diminished scales • incorporate exotic scales such as Hungarian major and Gypsy minor • and much more!

00695563 Book/CD Pack...$14.95

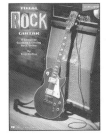

TOTAL ROCK GUITAR
INCLUDES TAB

A COMPLETE GUIDE TO LEARNING ROCK GUITAR
by Troy Stetina

This unique and comprehensive source for learning rock guitar is designed to develop both lead and rhythm playing. It covers: getting a tone that rocks • open chords, power chords and barre chords • riffs, scales and licks • string bending, strumming, palm muting, harmonics and alternate picking • all rock styles • and much more. The examples are in standard notation with chord grids and tab, and the CD includes full-band backing for all 22 songs.

00695246 Book/CD Pack...$17.95

GUITAR *signature licks*

Signature Licks book/CD packs provide a step-by-step breakdown of "right from the record" riffs, licks, and solos so you can jam along with your favorite bands. They contain performance notes and an overview of each artist's or group's style, with note-for-note transcriptions in notes and tab. The CDs feature full-band demos at both normal and slow speeds.

BEST OF ACOUSTIC GUITAR
00695640 ....$19.95

AEROSMITH 1973-1979
00695106 ....$22.95

AEROSMITH 1979-1998
00695219 ....$22.95

BEST OF AGGRO-METAL
00695592 ....$19.95

BEST OF CHET ATKINS
00695752 ....$22.95

THE BEACH BOYS DEFINITIVE COLLECTION
00695683 ....$22.95

BEST OF THE BEATLES FOR ACOUSTIC GUITAR
00695453 ....$22.95

THE BEATLES BASS
00695283 ....$22.95

THE BEATLES FAVORITES
00695096 ....$24.95

THE BEATLES HITS
00695049 ....$24.95

BEST OF GEORGE BENSON
00695418 ....$22.95

BEST OF BLACK SABBATH
00695249 ....$22.95

BEST OF BLINK - 182
00695704 ....$22.95

BEST OF BLUES GUITAR
00695846 ....$19.95

BLUES GUITAR CLASSICS
00695177 ....$19.95

BLUES/ROCK GUITAR MASTERS
00695348 ....$19.95

BEST OF CHARLIE CHRISTIAN
00695584 ....$22.95

BEST OF ERIC CLAPTON
00695038 ....$24.95

ERIC CLAPTON – THE BLUESMAN
00695040 ....$22.95

ERIC CLAPTON – FROM THE ALBUM UNPLUGGED
00695250 ....$24.95

BEST OF CREAM
00695251 ....$22.95

DEEP PURPLE – GREATEST HITS
00695625 ....$22.95

THE BEST OF DEF LEPPARD
00696516 ....$22.95

THE DOORS
00695373 ....$22.95

FAMOUS ROCK GUITAR SOLOS
00695590 ....$19.95

BEST OF FOO FIGHTERS
00695481 ....$22.95

GREATEST GUITAR SOLOS OF ALL TIME
00695301 ....$19.95

BEST OF GRANT GREEN
00695747 ....$22.95

GUITAR INSTRUMENTAL HITS
00695309 ....$19.95

GUITAR RIFFS OF THE '60S
00695218 ....$19.95

BEST OF GUNS N' ROSES
00695183 ....$22.95

HARD ROCK SOLOS
00695591 ....$19.95

JIMI HENDRIX
00696560 ....$24.95

HOT COUNTRY GUITAR
00695580 ....$19.95

BEST OF JAZZ GUITAR
00695586 ....$24.95

ERIC JOHNSON
00699317 ....$22.95

ROBERT JOHNSON
00695264 ....$22.95

THE ESSENTIAL ALBERT KING
00695713 ....$22.95

B.B. KING – THE DEFINITIVE COLLECTION
00695635 ....$22.95

THE KINKS
00695553 ....$22.95

BEST OF KISS
00699413 ....$22.95

MARK KNOPFLER
00695178 ....$22.95

BEST OF YNGWIE MALMSTEEN
00695669 ....$22.95

BEST OF PAT MARTINO
00695632 ....$22.95

MEGADETH
00695041 ....$22.95

WES MONTGOMERY
00695387 ....$22.95

BEST OF NIRVANA
00695483 ....$24.95

THE OFFSPRING
00695852 ....$24.95

VERY BEST OF OZZY OSBOURNE
00695431 ....$22.95

BEST OF JOE PASS
00695730 ....$22.95

PINK FLOYD – EARLY CLASSICS
00695566 ....$22.95

THE POLICE
00695724 ....$22.95

THE GUITARS OF ELVIS
00696507 ....$22.95

BEST OF QUEEN
00695097 ....$22.95

BEST OF RAGE AGAINST THE MACHINE
00695480 ....$22.95

RED HOT CHILI PEPPERS
00695173 ....$22.95

RED HOT CHILI PEPPERS – GREATEST HITS
00695828 ....$24.95

BEST OF DJANGO REINHARDT
00695660 ....$22.95

BEST OF ROCK
00695884 ....$19.95

BEST OF ROCK 'N' ROLL GUITAR
00695559 ....$19.95

BEST OF ROCKABILLY GUITAR
00695785 ....$19.95

THE ROLLING STONES
00695079 ....$22.95

BEST OF JOE SATRIANI
00695216 ....$22.95

BEST OF SILVERCHAIR
00695488 ....$22.95

THE BEST OF SOUL GUITAR
00695703 ....$19.95

BEST OF SOUTHERN ROCK
00695703 ....$19.95

ROD STEWART
00695663 ....$22.95

BEST OF SYSTEM OF A DOWN
00695788 ....$22.95

STEVE VAI
00673247 ....$22.95

STEVE VAI – ALIEN LOVE SECRETS: THE NAKED VAMPS
00695223 ....$22.95

STEVE VAI – FIRE GARDEN: THE NAKED VAMPS
00695166 ....$22.95

STEVE VAI – THE ULTRA ZONE: NAKED VAMPS
00695684 ....$22.95

STEVIE RAY VAUGHAN
00699316 ....$24.95

THE GUITAR STYLE OF STEVIE RAY VAUGHAN
00695155 ....$24.95

BEST OF THE VENTURES
00695772 ....$19.95

THE WHO
00695561 ....$22.95

BEST OF ZZ TOP
00695738 ....$22.95

Complete descriptions and songlists online!

FOR MORE INFORMATION, SEE YOUR LOCAL MUSIC DEALER, OR WRITE TO:

HAL•LEONARD® CORPORATION
7777 W. BLUEMOUND RD. P.O. BOX 13819 MILWAUKEE, WI 53213
www.halleonard.com
Prices, contents and availability subject to change without notice.

0606